Testimonials

"There's much to learn from it"

A great guide. It's quick and easy-to-use, and it touches y~~ ~~ first it seems specifically addressed to parenting children with autism but it should be read by ALL parents to solve common problems we face with children nowadays. Patience and communication seem to be the keywords! There's much to learn from it.

Patty Liberti
Teacher (trained and practising in Special Needs) & parent

"Extremely approachable"

As a young person who has grown up facing the challenges of a world that does not understand ASD, 'Dos and Don'ts' is a welcome manual of advice. Very readable and comprehensive, this book would be an excellent starting point for families learning to support autistic children. I sincerely hope that parents who are struggling to understand their autistic children will educate themselves through books like this, and avoid causing unintentional trauma and stress to their children.

Filled with innumerable hints and funny cartoons, 'Dos and Don'ts' is extremely approachable, and would be an effective and practical guide for any family adjusting to an ASD diagnosis.

Felicity*
17 years old, ASD, Australia

"Yay, fantastic!"

Initial thoughts are 'Yay, fantastic'... what a super job you have done in creating such a positive, helpful, and useful book! I can see and feel all through how this is underpinned by wanting things to feel easier for people who would be assessed/diagnosed on the autistic spectrum. It is also great to see that you have included the section on Trauma, as this is the area of my expertise (working on the neurological connections between body/brain/feelings/thoughts/emotions/connection with people, animals, and nature/physical play and movements).

Tamzin Baxter
Project Worker (Trauma Recovery)
Early Years Lead Practitioner (also qualified in Family Therapy)

"I recognised loads of situations"

This is a brilliant wee book. I wish I had this advice when my family were growing up!

I absolutely love the illustrations and I recognised loads of situations that we as a family experienced. My children are now all young adults (my youngest was diagnosed with ASD at 13). Even if you think your child could be 'on the spectrum' use these tips to provide more structure and support in day-to-day life (easier said than done!). I think this could be a great little bible of how to promote a positive family life. Katy clearly has great insight and above all I like the emphasis on maintaining low stress and minimising the impact of over stimulation. Children with Asperger's pick up very easily on stress from adults. It can become a downward spiral if there is not the right intervention.

I think on the whole it is very practical good advice that reflects the realities of living with autism in families. I think the part on trauma and school refusing is very important to recognise in teenagers. I like the promotion of a very useful 'trauma' check list that every educational psychologist should read.

I would definitely recommend this to parents, teachers and any professionals working with families affected by Autism.

Jane Catlin
Parent, Scotland

"Rigorously researched"

This book is much needed. It's quick and light, but rigorously researched and full of pointers to further key educational and developmental research.

MJ Kinnear
Teacher & researcher, UK

"This guide will help parents"

I liked all of the do and don't tips (I especially like #46 on the don't list!). I think this guide will help parents be Sweet Peas towards their autistic children.

CockneyRebel*, Bank Worker, UK
Diagnosed with Asperger's

"For parents ready to receive it, one key tip or strategy could change their kids' lives"

I have autistic traits, and I'm also blind. There were definitely situations in Katy's book that I recognized from my childhood.

I believe that the viewpoints you've shared are very useful. To clarify, their usefulness comes from considering the child's perspective in the moment... adults can get really focused on coping with their own everyday parental joys and challenges, as well as their worries for their children in the long term. Maybe sometimes, they might forget the in-the-moment understanding of their children's experiences that Katy's book brings.

For parents ready to receive it, one key tip or strategy could change their kids' lives.

Data4B*, Writer, USA

"Relevant and applicable"

Although this book aims to provide advice for those looking after an autistic child specifically, it can in fact can be relevant and applicable to anybody. As an 18-year-old student, I was still able to take almost every piece of advice and apply it to all of my social interactions with younger children (of which there are many in my life), but also, on occasion, to interaction with people of all ages.

I think it is easy to forget that small activities like these combine to make a large impact on the development of a child. The book acknowledges that what is often seen as 'not a big deal' really does have strong and lasting effects on children.

Eve Francis
Trainee teacher & professional babysitter

"Affirmations"

Warm fuzzy feeling inside – a lot of affirmations of what I thought, but I was looking outwards rather than inwards towards acceptance. Brilliant way of presenting this, Katy. I'd also like to say well done and thanks to you and your family, for pushing yourselves to do this for others when you didn't have to.

Omar Saleh
High school teacher & parent

*Pseudonyms and comments have been reproduced here with permission

Then come the questions -

Disclaimer

This work is based on my observations at first hand, accompanied by reading a great many books and articles, and by extensive online research. I have been much influenced by what has been said by older autistic people – teenagers and adults – about their experiences both of their current lives and their early years.

My main qualifications for writing this book are not formally impressive: I wrote it as a parent and as someone who shows a number of autistic traits herself, and therefore could be said to understand (at least to some small extent) some of the experiences autistic children might have.

Confession

So as a parent, have I managed to consistently do, and not do, all the things in this book that I've listed as being helpful and not-so-helpful?

No, most certainly I haven't (and don't)! This book actually started as my own list of notes for myself, to try to do things right and helpfully, instead of in ways that clearly made things worse. And I still need it, embarrassingly often.

Acknowledgements

Without the loving support, encouragement, inspiration and feedback of my husband, my mother and my sister I could not have done this; neither the supportive parenting nor the book.

Also I want to thank our wonderful 'educazione parentale' group here in Italy; the loving and positive attitude of the parents (now among my closest friends) and their children (now among my children's closest friends).

And finally let me thank my children's teacher, Andju, who my kids inform me is 'the only grown-up who really knows how to play'.

And introducing ...

Fuzzy, our hero (the creation of Matt Friedman, the illustrator of this book[i]), without whom it would all be ... well, just a bunch of words!

---

i Also the author of the book *Dude, I'm an Aspie! – Thoughts and Illustrations on Living with Asperger's Syndrome*, and the website and blog www.dudeimanaspie.com

What's outside my door today, d'you think?

Dos and Don'ts, Autism and Asperger's

Contents

For those using the book as a reference guide

To use this book as quick reference for specific issues (which you might already be aware of), the best method is to turn straight to the Index on page 85, where themes are listed alphabetically.

Introduction

This list suggests practical ways in which children, in particular those who have a predisposition towards autism, can be helped and supported (and not hindered) in becoming the best version of themselves, and in building the self-determination and confidence necessary to live full and happy lives. It does not give advice on how to cope with the more extreme symptoms and problems associated with autism[i].

A lot of the advice given is relevant for all ages, but overall it is most relevant for younger children (from babyhood to about 10 years old). This is because my children are still young and therefore, though I have read a great deal, I lack direct experience of living with teenagers. Watch this space.

The list is really not intended to be followed in a strict way, or to create feelings of inadequacy and guilt if you don't manage to change or to do things 'right'. My intention was rather to be as supportive and encouraging as possible to both parents and children. Whatever the scenario, it is just as important to be forgiving and kind towards yourself as to those around you! If you feel at times that you're not coping, I think these feelings are only too natural. We all need help, support and understanding from others; people are simply not designed to be parents in isolation. I believe this is why we have such a strong instinct to reach out to others, in person and through books.

Finally, let me add that I do not think that these are by any means the *only* ways to manage, or deal with specific situations. Everybody is different and there are bound to be many other ways of doing things that would work equally well (if not better!) in some cases. Furthermore, there will of course be any number of scenarios that have not been covered here.

---

i   If you are struggling with more extreme symptoms and problems, and overwhelming practical problems associated with day-to-day life, besides seeking help from family and friends and any local support groups (e.g. parents' groups), you should also seek assistance from the welfare and health systems of wherever you live, if you have not already done so.

Do

1. Provide unconditional love and approval. This does not mean being permissive: you can model how to behave, and have rules, without conditionally giving or taking away approval.

2. Nurture beneficial relationships.

3. Avoid competitive situations, or situations where anyone is compared unfavourably with anyone else.

4. Avoid situations where your child feels intense pressure to conform or pretend in order to be accepted by others.

5. Keep artificial lights not-too-bright (using dimmer switches or low-output bulbs). Avoid using fluorescent light bulbs.

6. Make sure there is access to somewhere quiet and calming, on demand (if you are in a city, you can find calm and quiet in public gardens, libraries, or museums and art galleries).

7. Spend plenty of quiet contemplative time; quiet time for your child to work on their own projects, time in nature away from shops, noise, traffic and artificial stimuli.

8. Spend time with animals. If your life allows for its continued care, consider adopting a dog or cat, or even just a

hamster or guinea pig. A larger pet can however also be good for sleeping with at night, to offer company and reassurance (apply flea drops regularly, preferably natural ones).

9. Spend time in outdoor noncompetitive, non-structured activities e.g. biking, swimming, climbing, ice-skating, sledging, walking, horse-riding, fishing, boating, and camping together with friends or family.

10. Find play parks with lots of space and few people (or go at times when they're quiet). Swings, see-saws, roundabouts, climbing frames, slides and trampolines[i] are great fun, and exercise too.

11. Travel. Consider camping or renting a cabin in places you love: even just for a few days it can be a refreshing change. We prefer woods and lakes to Disneyland (it's also cheaper), but you can focus on your own family's preferences, so wherever you all feel relaxed and happy. Avoid being in a hurry or being goal-oriented. Take time to observe your surroundings and be together, bring along your child's book and your own, and maybe a pack of cards and some binoculars.

Free! Free!

12. Regularly arrange to see friends and relatives (maybe giving priority to those you and your family find kind and unstressful).

13. Nurture your child's interests – perhaps building, science, music, art, or looking after animals and plants. If your child has

---

i   There are some types of movement that seem to be particularly good; often trampolining, and other activities that involve jumping or spinning around can give great enjoyment and satisfaction.

a special interest, see what you can do to help locate resources and mentors for them[i].

14. Let your child wear clothes they find comfortable, and if they have sensory problems, you can order seamless socks online and cut out labels from clothes[ii].

15. Provide lots of sensory play for young children using sand, water, earth, playdough or clay, materials and fabrics, art supplies (e.g. large rolls of paper and large bottles of washable paint)[iii].

---

i   You may notice a link between your child's anxiety levels and how much time they want to spend on their special interest. It seems that the special interest (or at times it may seem like an 'obsessive' interest!) serves another important purpose besides just plain enjoyment (which it however also clearly provides): to maintain emotional equilibrium in stressful times. For example, my son can use his strong interest in cars to help him to diffuse his stress after challenging social situations (we walk around the car park comparing all the car models and their maximum speeds, literally until he's happy again). It's clear to me how important an intense involvement in one's special interest can be for wellbeing and equilibrium during certain phases in life, since I have a rather strong tendency towards having what my husband might well call 'obsessive' interests myself.

If your child's special interest looks like it's literally becoming an obsession, to the exclusion of other important things in life, I'd recommend starting with concentrating on ways (some of which are described in this book) in which you can work on *reducing anxiety levels*. You may find that if you succeed in doing that, your child's level of engagement in their special interest will naturally decline to a manageable level. Having said that, if their special interest has any detrimental effects on themselves or others, you'll need to apply some redirection. For more help on this, Tony Attwood (see the Reading List) is very informative and helpful on the topic, dedicating a whole chapter to it in his *Complete Guide to Asperger's*.

ii   It can feel like real torture for an autistic child to wear uncomfortable clothes.

iii For small children, being allowed to make their own playdough can be really fun, with white flour, salt, water, and food colourings (Tip: add the colours to the water in a glass, it works best and it looks lovely). Besides being a great way to learn about mixing colours, the dough feels and smells nice, and it's often played with for hours afterwards (store it in a bag in the fridge).

16. Provide lots of creative, sensory, hands-on experience in everyday living. Even very small children can help with baking, cooking and gardening (don't be too fussy about the results!).

17. Respect preferences expressed by your child where you can, even if they don't make any sense to you (e.g. not getting head wet under the shower – why not wash in the bathtub instead? Or refusing to wear jeans, or the expensive shoes you bought – why not stick with jogging trousers and sneakers?)[i].

18. Whenever possible, give a good few minutes' warning before changing setting e.g. leaving the house, leaving a playground, the beach etc. (making sure you get an answer confirming they got the message – if they're concentrating on something else they may not have heard a word you said!). Try to also give a few minutes' warning before mealtimes, or anything else what will require changing activity.

19. At breakfast each morning (or in another appropriate moment and setting, depending on your family's habits), try to dedicate a few moments to looking together at the overall plans for the day. Making a pictorial calendar with/for your child can also be of enormous benefit (at the moment the 'monthly planner' format works best for us)[ii].

---

i   Consider your priorities, and decide which specific areas you really need to be firm in. This will leave you to be flexible on other areas that you find less important. If you're firm on everything, you'll only end up totally exhausted, plus having your children live in dread of the sound of your voice. My personal area of greatest firmness is kindness and consideration towards others. This includes helping out those in need and trying to make amends if someone's hurt (or at least always making sure to check if they're okay), while I'm not very strict on others, e.g. neatness or table manners (except if we're at a wedding or in a nice restaurant, or at someone's house for whom that's important), or making annoying noises, or playing messy games, though sometimes I might ask the kids to take those last two outside into the garden.

ii   It's worth noting here that children don't need anywhere near so much warning about *positive* activities that they don't find scary in any way. While those they may find difficult may need days of repeated reminders and emotional preparation.

20. Give unlimited access to physical affection[i] (essential for small children and infants, though important for all ages, depending on demand!).

21. Take plenty of time over bedtime, with lots of reading and being cosy together. Your child may need this time to settle down and process the day's events – I notice a strong link with how socially stimulating the day has been, and how long bedtime becomes[ii]. Avoid trying to make your child fall asleep alone if they don't feel ready for that, and give them all the cuddles and physical contact they need – in our family this closeness and attention at night actually seems essential in order to achieve emotional equilibrium during the day[iii].

Really?

Yes.

22. Make sure your child has access to you during the night (and is close enough for you to hear and respond if they need you), as night is the time when they might feel most isolated and insecure.

23. In infancy, often the easiest sleeping arrangement is having a cot with one side taken off alongside the parents' bed – this way

---

i   Note the 'access to'. This is important as your child may not be comfortable with *unsolicited* shows of affection.

ii This may be the time, when relaxed, that your child starts to talk about things, or ask you questions, that reveal their state of mind and provide you with valuable information.

iii We've found that back scratches and massages can play an important role in calming down an overexcited or upset child. Our son also has a thing about lying full length on top of me or his papa, or having me lie on him, when he's feeling overwhelmed or distressed. While I'm a bit worried about squashing him flat, could this be the 'deep pressure' that Temple Grandin talks about (see Reading List)?

Do

you can get to each other simply by rolling over, so it's less likely you'll hurt your back or get cross, or walk into the wall. This way you don't even need to properly wake up, let alone get up!

24. When your baby gets older and more agile, consider going straight on to a proper child's bed, with just a low barrier to prevent falling out. This way your child can climb in and out of their own bed (making them much happier about the whole idea), and you can lie down next to them in their bed when reading or comforting, so no uncomfortable crouching over cribs or back-breaking acrobatics trying to get them in and out.

25. Avoid places where overstimulation is likely. For example, shopping malls, supermarkets, and any other crowded, noisy places with artificial lights and little natural green or sky. Try to go shopping and out for other activities at times when few people are around, even if that mcans changing your routines. Be relaxed, take time, involve your child (they could find items on the list, push the trolley, choose the fruit, etc.).

26. Avoid running errands with your child when you are tired and stressed yourself, or in a rush. This kind of situation could easily end in meltdown.

27. Learn to recognise the signs of over-stimulation (distress signals – you know your own child best, but they could be anything from high pitched noises to repetitive movements or tics), and change environment as quickly and calmly as possible.

28. Allow stimming[i] (hand flapping, making noises, rocking, and other repetitive actions) do not try to impede it, or in fact criticise it at all. It's essential for self-regulation, and will also provide useful clues for you about your child's state of mind, allowing you to act accordingly.

29. Help your child when they ask you to, wherever possible, even if you don't understand why, or you do not think that what they are asking for help with is important. If you do this by default, you will find that when you ask for help in return, they will usually comply quite willingly[ii].

30. When being asked questions, in particular repetitive ones, be patient. If they ask the same question and seem

---

i   Self-stimulation. It has been pointed out to me by an autistic friend that a problem with being allowed to stim unimpeded can be the social stigma and judgement attached. Good point – maybe one can try overall to avoid situations/places where people are unfriendly and intolerant (even when things are explained to them), and certainly to make sure your child is not going to be at the mercy of those people? Thankfully it seems that overall (thanks to parents and autistic people speaking out to raise awareness and bring about change, and to initiatives like Sesame Street and *Our Amazing Children*) understanding about autism is growing, and with it tolerance.

ii   You will then not need to resort to threatening punishment or offering rewards. You may have already found these more coercive techniques to be problematic, often turning out to be quite ineffectual in the long term or for cultivating self-motivation. Personally I have found they are not very effective in the short term either as (with autistic kids in particular) they often don't seem to produce quite the intended results!

fully satisfied with hearing the answer over and over, they may be checking in with their reality to feel secure. However, if they register frustration when you answer, you may well be talking at cross-purposes. Instead of repeating the same answer over and over, try considering the question a little and what the child might actually mean. It may be that you are not answering the question they are attempting to ask you[i].

31. Be open, supportive and positive about your child's autism, which will lead to them feeling confident about it and about who they are. It is important that their challenges are addressed in a neutral way, and refusal to talk on the subject reinforces the idea that the child is alone in their struggles, and that having autism is somehow a terrible thing.

Me...

me...,

oh, that is SO me!

I rock!

32. Help your child find positive information and resources about autism.

33. Follow leads on your child's own passions, build on their strengths, and assist them in finding places and people where

---

i   An example of this is my son asking about the treatment of animals. He asks, for example 'WHY do they keep chickens in factories?', and I answer 'so that they can sell them in supermarkets' (I was explaining to him why we don't usually buy meat from our supermarket). Two minutes later, 'yes but WHY do they keep them in factories?' We could continue going round in circles like this for a long time, and I could get exasperated, or assume he's not very bright. But perhaps what he is actually asking me is 'how could anyone, ever, do such a thing?', so when I instead answer 'it is awful, isn't it – but luckily more and more people realise this and try not to support it by not buying the meat', he seems satisfied and later says to me 'can we buy all the chicks from the factory, and set them free?'.

they feel at home. Avoid making them do activities they don't like and aren't good at[i].

34. Get a set of noise-cancelling headphones in case of unavoidable noisy situations (on an aeroplane, for example).

35. Have a pair of sunglasses handy for your child to wear if they find it's too bright.

---

i   I find questionable the much-applied idea that it is somehow character-building to be forced to do things you don't enjoy and aren't good at. I have found Alfie Kohn's work particularly informative on this (see Reading List), and his work on motivation and self-motivation is backed up with a great deal of research evidence.

On the other hand what is clearly shown to be character-building, is to have the opportunity to find goals you really want to achieve, and then to see that the way to get there is though hard work and perseverance (even on parts that you may enjoy less than others). This is something that a person can truly learn only through their own volition – it is worth noting that even very small children will show an amazing talent for understanding and doing this, if they are given the chance to do so.

36. Avoid too much screen time by providing attractive alternatives, as too much time watching TV and films, and spent on computers, tablets or smart phones has an overstimulating effect[i]. Also, your child risks losing their self-entertaining skills[ii].

37. Avoid eating too often in restaurants or cafes, especially crowded noisy ones. Maybe bring a picnic instead, so you can eat somewhere quiet where you don't have to 'behave'.

38. Provide healthy and regular meals. Good nutrition is fundamental to emotional well-being, especially for those who can be extremely sensitive to physical discomfort. Many people

---

i   I realise this may get a lot harder to do as your children get older. However, you can still take the lead on fun outdoors activities, games, reading and audiobooks, outings and so on. Also arrange regular holidays or at least weekends away, with no electronic devices or screens.

ii   If your child often complains about being bored, look at their screen time, and also at how much influence they have over important decisions affecting their own life. The article *Boredom* by Perri Klass, Harvard Medicine online journal (https://hms.harvard.edu/harvard-medicine/adventure-issue/boredom), gives some interesting insights.

have found that there are times when supplementing a healthy diet with certain minerals, vitamins or tonics can be beneficial[i].

39. Give priority to nurturing a couple of key friendships, following your child's lead and observing who they really connect with and who they have a positive relationship with. Enlarge the circle of friends by all means, but with care and taking it slowly. Observe closely and listen to your child about what constellations of friends they like best. When they feel confident within a small circle of good, loyal friends (they may

Company.

A crowd.

Crowd-ed.

Get me out of here!

---

i   There is a lot of literature available on this – and it certainly makes sense that deficiencies can contribute to physical and psychological stress. You can observe through trying them if your child benefits from certain supplements. However, if supplementing is done obsessively or taken to excess, and certainly if it's expected to be some kind of panacea, it seems fairly likely this could have a negative impact both on the emotional equilibrium of the parents and on the family budget.

at first prefer to see one friend at a time[i]), they are much more likely to eventually be able to interact happily and confidently in more diverse group situations[ii]. For older kids, also finding pen-friends with similar interests can be a good idea.

40. When your younger children meet new kids, observe how things are going. If anyone is in difficulties, you can intervene with some optional, noncompetitive activities or games[iii], or by reading a story, and/or also just spend a little time yourself playing or chatting (gently and unobtrusively) with any child who feels hurt, frustrated or left out.

---

i   In school situations, obsessive clinging to one friend as a point of reference can be common. If you consider how overwhelmed and insecure your child might be feeling, and their propensity for one-on-one interacting, you can start to see why. Nurturing an additional friendship can therefore be helpful in this situation, as it is better not to have all your eggs in one basket! However only do this in a natural, no-pressure way, or you risk making your child feel more insecure.

You could help nurture additional friendships informally e.g. by creating opportunities during the holidays to get to know another schoolfellow who they like, or spending time with the child of close family friends, or a cousin, even if of a different age. Perhaps your child might also enjoy special interest clubs on topics they're keen on, though don't bank on this because unless it's a really small and/or gentle group they may find the social element stressful and prefer to follow up their special interests alone or with a like-minded mentor.

ii I don't think it is good for a sensitive child to be regularly exposed, against their wishes, to stressful competitive or hostile social situations from which they have no means of escape. Often in our well-meaning attempts to 'toughen up' our shy, sensitive children, frustratingly they seem to get even more anxious, fearful, and negative. I think it works well to use the child's own feeling about what they can manage as an overall guide; this way they're likely to grow stronger and more resilient in the long run. You can introduce new situations and challenges in steps you think your child can probably deal with. When trying any larger steps, make sure they are in situations you can both get out of easily, without any hassle or comments: observe closely what happens and you can adapt your strategy accordingly.

iii Maybe this could be called 'directing the dynamics', a bit like moving stones to get a stream going in the right direction. Soon (when the kids know each other and have settled into a natural positive dynamic) you will need to do very little, and eventually nothing at all. Children who find social situations daunting often find it easier at first to relate to others when there is some structure offered.

Oppan gangnam style!
Gangnam style!
Op, op, op, op...

41. Arrive early at parties. This allows time to become familiar with the environment, and means not being faced with an overwhelming crowd on arrival.

42. Help your child to find quiet space and time alone or just with a carer or friend, during parties or gatherings. Later they will know how to do this on their own.

Goodbye.

43. Aim to arrive early to appointments: leaving much more time usually means you won't be stressed when setting out, and the journey can be more pleasant (and possibly less dangerous) than otherwise.

44. Avoid being in a hurry. Allow lots of time, wherever you go, for meandering and exploring.

45. Try to not have too many time-constrained appointments. I think one a day is generally quite enough, and at least a couple of days a week it's pleasant to have none at all.

46. Live in the moment, take plenty of time to simply enjoy life. Take things slowly, *enjoy!*

47. Bring your book or a magazine on outings, or go in the company of a good friend, so you can sit down and enjoy the minutes you get while your children explore and play wherever they wish to (provided it's not the lion's pen at the zoo[i]). Stop in places with space to play, preferably in nature with no structured activities. Bring a flask of coffee or tea along ☺

48. Say how you feel (keeping it brief and relevant to the situation), even if you're cross or tired. It will be much easier for your child to then understand why and how you are acting, and to make observations about it and allowances for it. However, make sure you say it in a way which simply states facts rather than putting any blame or responsibility on anyone.

49. Gently and carefully, and only if it feels really natural and right (and while keeping a very open mind), you could try to help them identify their own more difficult emotions – try asking them gently and flexibly what feels like (also physically) and together think of what things/events might  have triggered it[ii]. Make it clear to them that you consider it legitimate and perfectly normal to feel that way in the circumstances[iii]. Keep on listening to them, and stop talking if they ask you to, or if they're looking blank.

---

i   Though knowing my son, they might be just fine in there. No, that's a joke, please don't try it !!!

ii   Maybe meltdowns are rarely truly about the thing that apparently caused them, like being served a hated meal or having to leave the house. Isn't it more likely to be about deeper things e.g. not feeling safe, sensing stress or conflict, lack of control, habitually not being informed or consulted, or feeling misunderstood/judged?

iii Negating or judging others' feelings is counter-productive, as you can't change how they feel simply by thinking it's unreasonable. There are ALWAYS legitimate reasons for feelings, even when the 'why' of them is not fully known or understood.

50. Try making affectionate animal noises (purring for example) when your child spontaneously caresses and hugs you. It can be sweet and funny, while being both encouraging and unthreatening.

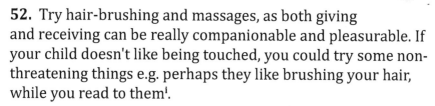

51. Try nose-touching (touching your noses together) if your child is not keen on kisses.

52. Try hair-brushing and massages, as both giving and receiving can be really companionable and pleasurable. If your child doesn't like being touched, you could try some non-threatening things e.g. perhaps they like brushing your hair, while you read to them[i].

53. Try some yoga! We are lucky enough to have a wonderful teacher, and a class with our closest friends. We do things like being animals or travelling to places by different means of transport, and doing poses like 'the bunk' or 'the turtle', which mean (usually) parent underneath, and children in order of size balancing on top! I'm always amazed it's possible. There's a lot of laughing ☺. My son now asks me almost every evening for the following exercise: he lies on his back on a soft blanket, I take first his feet in my hands and lift them a little off the ground, move them in small circles, and then wiggle and shake them gently for a while, then the same but with the arms and finally very gently lifting and moving the head a little way from side to side and gently massaging the neck (he often starts giggling then). The person should try to relax completely. I'm not saying this is for everyone, but you might find similar things that are really relaxing, feel good, and involve your child being fully in their body and trusting another person. Follow your child's lead on what *they* enjoy, and follow their instructions when they say 'more', 'less', 'higher', or 'ow, stop!'.

Drama/theatre games and activities might also be enjoyed, and can be useful for practising different roles, conversations and situations.

---

i   I think it is much less scary for them this way as a) they are the proactive one, fully in control of the situation and b) your attention is not focused on them.

54. Explain certain traits to others e.g. that if they have to say your child's name ten times to get their attention, it's nothing personal. Or that it's necessary for your child to drape themselves around you and stay there, when they begin to feel socially overwhelmed. Or that being touched and physically manipulated without their consent is not something they are likely to respond well to[i]. When people are given the chance to understand, they're more likely to be tolerant and to like and accept your child for who they are.

AARRRGHH!

55. If your toddler hates being belted in, try to find strategies that make it easier for them. High chairs and prams/strollers are less important, as it's usually possible to find ways around having to firmly strap your child in. But if you're having trouble with the car seat, try giving your child as much autonomy as you can, as early as possible. The more they feel in control (climbing in, clipping themselves in), the happier they will be with the idea. You can also try to make the whole 'going in the car' thing a positive experience. I used to pack little picnic boxes for my kids, to eat in the car once we were on the way. They loved it[ii].

56. Be patient and tolerant where you can, try to ask yourself what the child's intentions were before getting annoyed, or what stimulus they might be responding to[iii].

57. If your child's attempts at social interaction are unusual, be accepting of them and try to encourage others to do the same. This will help your child to become more confident in making

---

i   It may be necessary to explain that one to, for example, a gymnastics teacher.

ii   Though my husband drew the line at hard-boiled eggs...

iii   It is no coincidence that your child suddenly becomes more demanding and impossible in exactly the moment when everyone is getting stressed, or worried, or hurrying. Being sensitive, your child is probably sensing and reproducing the emotions that are circulating around them.

I come in peace!

Yeah yeah yeah, c'mon, "ET," let's get some lunch.

further attempts. If appropriate, you can also advise them on good ways of interaction by telling them how people are likely to feel or respond to them when they say or do certain things.

58. During conversation with your child, listen to their interests and opinions (even if they seem weird to you). Try responding in a curious, uncritical way, and make an effort to avoid bringing the topic around to what *you* think they should be interested in or learning about. You might find that you learn new and interesting things during these chats.

59. Make it clear to your child that it's fine if they do not always wish to return gestures of affection from adults[i].

Just wanna see that beautiful face!

---

i   Frankly I find it a little strange how we think that children should accept embracing, kissing, patting and general handling from adults in all kinds of situations, and not just from adults they don't know very well, but even from some they don't know at all! Personally I would not enjoy this, and I think our children should know that they also are free to reject it. You may need to actively support them in this, as often children's feelings are not taken very seriously by adults. However, remember that people's intentions are nearly always kind, so when you say 'I'm afraid that my son/daughter does not generally like being kissed/touched by people they don't know very well', do it in as friendly a way as possible, to try to avoid giving too much offence.

60. Leave your child in peace when you sense they are withdrawing (by this I do not mean banishing them, or giving them 'time out'); gently tell them that you are available when they need you, and if possible stay within sight, physically present but getting on with your daily tasks e.g. cooking, reading, working etc. No need to bother your child

with any questions or demands right now, though you could in between make unobtrusive gestures like putting a drink or snack to hand, or tucking a blanket around them if it's cold. Maybe offer to read to them, or to accompany or help them in any preferred game, when you sense that they are feeling a bit better. If they refuse just say in a neutral tone 'Okay. You know I'm here if you need me'.

Whee –hee-hee!
Gleefully glad
to be me!

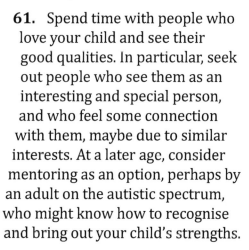

61. Spend time with people who love your child and see their good qualities. In particular, seek out people who see them as an interesting and special person, and who feel some connection with them, maybe due to similar interests. At a later age, consider mentoring as an option, perhaps by an adult on the autistic spectrum, who might know how to recognise and bring out your child's strengths.

62. Ask your children for help and collaboration with household tasks, and accept all forthcoming help cheerfully, going easy on suggestions and corrections. I find that leaving the room to go do something else is quite a good strategy, if I feel myself getting tense... and if you're anything like me you can also apply it when your partner changes the baby or loads the dishwasher. No need to apply any rewards or punishments for this, beyond the logical things like 'When we've cleaned up, we can go out!' or 'Just as soon as you guys have laid the table, we can eat'. I don't find it strictly necessary to assign specific chores to people (though at times it makes sense), because of the importance of flexibility. Recognising when other people need help and what with, and having the momentum to give that help spontaneously, seems an essential part of being a happy and active member of the family, and of the wider community too[i].

63. Try to approach exasperating situations with patience and humour. A bit of laughter makes everything, however hard, more palatable[ii].

64. Try to avoid stress/overload in your own life (or the former will be impossible!).

65. Do your best to model enjoyment of life and loving relationships. Take time, be kind, be contented, be loving, as much as you can be. If your life does not seem to permit these things, consider any ways you may be able to change things for the better, if it is within your power to do so![iii]

---

i   I really try to make sure everyone helps out in the house, mostly because I'm darned if I'm doing it all by myself! Also my mother pointed out that I wouldn't be doing my kids much good (in particular my daughter) by modelling how to be an exhausted drudge. By now, whenever I'm getting stressed because of being overloaded with too many tasks at once, instead of flapping about getting more and more overheated, I say 'Right, everyone. This is what needs doing', and we sit ourselves briefly down at the kitchen table and write out a list of tasks. My kids are now so used to this that they spontaneously come out with 'I'll make breakfast!', 'I'll feed the animals!', or whatever. I'd like to say that I don't believe in punishments and don't apply them, but I suppose me getting in a complete tizzy is probably considered punishment enough by my family, much as I hate the idea.

ii There was an earthquake in our area a week ago, at breakfast time. Afterwards our son said cheerfully 'the earthquake will have shaken the dew off the grass, so I can fly my remote control helicopter'. I find earthquakes terrifying, but this made even me laugh!

iii Though please don't feel guilty about the things you can't change! I know very well that there is not always the freedom to make lifestyle changes.

66. Make it clear that it's okay to change your mind, and model this by, when you do it yourself, giving a proper explanation (and an apology if appropriate) to those who may be affected by your change of heart. This is an essential skill, and will result in an adult who is strong in their beliefs but also flexible about listening to others' points of view, and in responding appropriately to changing circumstances.

67. Read a lot of books and comics together, and download your child's favourite audiobooks (for car journeys, etc.[i]). Do this in preference to films, which are overstimulating[ii] and don't usually allow for a freely roaming imagination. If you don't enjoy reading, try to find someone who does, and who the child likes to read with (or be read to). Reading is such a great skill for both independent research and for developing a powerful imagination. Stories and novels also stimulate empathy in both us and our children, as we live our way through the story from someone else's point of view.

68. Make up stories and songs about things. This is actually a great way of imparting knowledge (e.g. about geography, history, politics, art etc.), as for some reason, where a textbook might make us fall asleep after a few minutes, an adventuresome narrative has the power to keep us gripped for ages – and even remember some of the details afterwards!

69. Follow your own interests, showing your child how much you enjoy them – that is, the process itself, not just attaining goals. If it's a competitive hobby, show that you love it in itself and not just for the sake of winning.

---

i Though daydreaming is important too – an essential skill for any child. Games on the tablet or phone, and films, I think are therefore to be avoided when travelling, if at all possible (bearing in mind that your own sanity is of vital importance, so please go easy on yourself and take things step by step, sounding out the right moment if you're introducing new habits and ideas).

ii Especially if your child is overexposed to them. We usually watch a movie once a week, and on 'movie night' we choose the film together at dinner. Besides this, we sometimes watch documentaries (on space, nature, and all kinds of other topics), and an occasional recorded series. I would really avoid online viewing if at all possible, as unless you're incredibly vigilant, anything could happen.

70. Drink water, not soft drinks! Sugar and additives, especially in drinks, are very overstimulating, besides being bad for your teeth[i].

71. Try to eat healthily and regularly, and together. If your child gets bad-tempered, ask yourself if it's nearly a meal-time (many kids can burn up their fuel, seemingly almost completely, and suddenly go completely pale and feel awful... at which point it is time for some proper food, quick!).

72. Try to always have fresh fruit and water available, accessible for busy children to grab. Also other healthy snacks are an option (though maybe nothing too substantial if you don't want to risk ruining mealtimes). This is not to say you have to always avoid unhealthy foods, in fact I would highly recommend fun outings and ice-creams, or other delicious treats when enjoying yourselves together.

73. Be aware about allergies, keep an eye on your child's overall health and wellbeing (if they look pale, and/or often have a runny nose, nosebleeds, tummy pains, or other symptoms). You could try experimentally removing things you think may have a negative impact.

---

i   You might observe your child go completely wild and overexcited for a bit, then suddenly all pale and floppy.

Do

74. Be aware that any resistance encountered when washing, showering, cleaning teeth etc. could be due to sensory issues (water too cold? Toothpaste tastes unbearable? Soap getting too close to the eyes?), so do whatever you can to make the experience more pleasant. Also it's best to avoid leaving getting ready for bed till too late, when everyone's overtired[i].

75. Do lots of scientific experiments (you can get many great books and look up online, safe experiments that you can do at home). This helps your child to put together ideas about how the world works, how it looks and feels, what it's made of etc.

76. Change scene. When everyone's irritable, or not really enjoying life, just get out of the house! Go somewhere nice, take a picnic or grab something along the way.

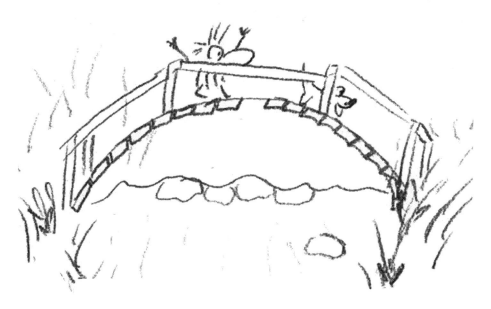

77. Try to keep your home reasonably tidy. It's best not to have too much stuff, as it's much easier (for everyone) to keep sane in a more minimalist environment. Try to avoid having too

---

i   Something that really works for us is, when reading a story (e.g. on the sofa in the living room), taking a break between chapters for changing into pyjamas, brushing teeth, etc. and then having the next chapter in bed. If you're watching a film, you could pause it and have an 'interval' for doing this.

many toys in bedrooms, or keep them in a way that you and/or your child can put things away easily in cupboards or boxes.

78. Consider decluttering your house. If you gave half your things away, you'd have double the space and a lot less to worry about! You may also benefit from doing toy-swaps with friends, especially for more bulky items. Kids are usually more excited about seeing fresh toys or ones they haven't seen for a while.

79. Provide access to musical instruments, and play favourite music at home and on journeys.

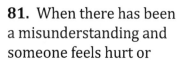

80. Dance together (and with your husband/wife and other siblings), to your favourite music. It's so much fun!

81. When there has been a misunderstanding and someone feels hurt or

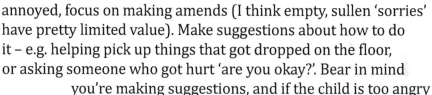

annoyed, focus on making amends (I think empty, sullen 'sorries' have pretty limited value). Make suggestions about how to do it – e.g. helping pick up things that got dropped on the floor, or asking someone who got hurt 'are you okay?'. Bear in mind you're making suggestions, and if the child is too angry or upset to follow through on them, never mind! Modelling being forgiving and understanding is what's important, and each time you do that it becomes more likely your child will follow suit. Avoid character judgements, laying blame, and holding grudges.

'oh dear.'

82. Treat your child with respect and consideration. Say 'sorry' with sincerity, if you did something wrong or hurtful (even without meaning to). I mean proper sorry, not 'sorry *you* feel that way'. Your child will then start saying sincerely 'sorry' to you, when they realise they did something that annoyed or hurt you.

83. If you get an 'inappropriate' response from your child, ask yourself about the context and what you really meant, or how you felt when saying it. Autistic children are not usually good at mixed messages. It seems to me that they often sense and respond to the true sentiment behind the talking (and show an almost allergic reaction to manipulative practices); they generally don't parrot social niceties or just go along with the charade! So, if your child responds to you in a seemingly odd or irrelevant way, consider the possibility that they may be responding to the other side of a mixed message or an unintentional undercurrent of feelings from you, or others present.

84. Let your child communicate within the family in their own way (also non-verbally). Don't insist on the use of words, if you in any case understand what they mean. Intentionally misunderstanding or refusing to understand can inflict unnecessary emotional trauma. Your child is more likely to learn how to effectively communicate with others if you give them secure foundations of self-confidence on which to build. Later you can make suggestions (preferably when solicited) about how to be understood by others, and how words can be used, although you may well find that it is unnecessary as they will learn through their own observations. If your child is non-speaking, look into using FC[i], which many autistic people have reported to have found very helpful.

85. Go ahead and give some of your child's teddies and toy animals characters and voices (pretend, initiated by you ☺). They can often be really useful in providing funny, unthreatening love, reassurance, friendship (e.g. in cases where

---

i   Facilitated Communication. Ralph James Savarese gives an account of his family's experiences using FC in his book *Reasonable People: A Memoir of Autism and Adoption*, a part of which has been written independently by his autistic son.

a child has been very traumatised by experiences with real people and needs to develop basic trust again), and can also sometimes be a channel for your child to bring out and work through feelings of anger, frustration and hurt[i].

86. Make it clear you will support your child in situations where they are being judged, put down, or sold short by others, even other grown-ups, *even* grown ups in positions of authority.

... uhhhhh ...

87. Try to be understanding about your child sometimes not paying attention, and about forgetfulness. It's not intentional! It may be annoying sometimes, but on the flipside you have a child who can REALLY concentrate on things they're interested in.

88. Make spontaneous decisions together about doing fun things. Hey, why don't we go to the beach, or lake?? Yes, even with no towels or swimming things (if you happen to already be out)! Making-do not only means a lot less unpacking for you later, but it teaches a really important lesson. Enjoying life, taking some risks, being spontaneous... it's all part of living life to the full, and this is a controlled way of showing your child that everything will be fine – even without being properly prepared or having the right gear!

89. If plans change suddenly, give an explanation about what's happening. Even when very little, your child prefers to know what's going on; being consulted and informed gives them the feeling of control over their lives and leads to proactiveness and flexibility.

Oh! Well...

90. Set boundaries, in particular when people's actions might harm someone else. Having clear rules is a good

---

i I'd suggest sewing labels onto any teddies or toy animals your child is particularly attached to, with your phone number and a 'please return me!' message. We've learnt about this the hard way.

Do

way of doing this, and applying them firmly in moments when it becomes necessary[i].

---

i   In our family we have found that the ways of doing this that have worked best for us (thank you Adele Faber and Elaine Mazlish, see Reading List) are as follows:

a) State firmly what things are for e.g. 'Sand is not for throwing, it's for playing with!'. You can also give relevant information e.g. 'When it's thrown around it can go in people's eyes'. These things can be said loudly and firmly: you want to see that behaviour stop immediately. You could then state your expectation in a quieter tone e.g. 'I expect you to be able to play together gently'. Another thing I would add here is that when children begin to go wild and hurt one another, they are probably stressed or overstimulated, and it's likely someone feels either overwhelmed or hurt by the others and/or by the situation. Considering this, some positive redirecting could also be in order. You could initiate an alternative collaborative activity – 'Ooh, I know, we could dig a moat together and then fill it from the watering can. We could even make some paper boats to float on it!'. Though if a child has clearly just Had Enough, you can also see if they'd like to come in with you to have a story, or a drink or snack, or another quiet game you know they like. When they're older they'll know how to seek some quiet time and space by themselves.

b) On roughhousing, I'd keep a very close eye on this. At any point when something looks painful or even just very unequal (e.g. more children jumping on just one child, or a bigger child wrestling a much smaller one to the ground), even if they are all laughing, I step in and say 'WAIT A SECOND! David (example name), are you enjoying this game?'. If the answer from the crushed or chased child is 'No' (even a shake of the head), I say firmly and loudly 'Games are only fun when EVERYONE enjoys it. If there is any person not enjoying it, it's NOT A FUN GAME anymore'. If the child say yes it *is* fun (this can just as easily happen), confirming positively that they are in fact enjoying the game, then I let them continue. Sometimes however before letting them go on playing (especially if the game involves people saying 'stop, stop, no, NO!' between shrieks of laughter) I get them to agree on a word for when someone REALLY means 'stop!'. When that word is said, the other players know they're serious, and it must be respected.

c) State the rules firmly e.g. 'No hitting'. I have found myself literally standing between children who are trying to hit or kick one another, at which point it can get a bit silly, especially if I was baking and have really sticky hands. However outside moments of *extremis* I emphasise that we *never* use violence, and that if you're upset with someone it's much better to tell them what's up, and also try to think and explain why (to give that person a chance to change whatever it is that upset you). If the child feels unable to do that, or the situation continues to upset them even after they do speak up, they should come and find me (or whichever grown up is around).

d) During hard times, when it seems that treating others badly becomes a regular occurrence, you can sit down together as a family and make a big poster called 'Family Rules'. Let the children write down their important rules too, and illustrate it together. Thankfully we are no longer in a condition that requires this measure, but it has really worked for us in the past. The main themes were 'No name-calling or verbal abuse' and 'No violence of any kind'. The children's final contribution at the time was 'Grown ups: No shouting!'. Hmm.

91. If your child has a tendency to be autocratic (to try and dictate to you and other family members what to do and how to do it, and not to seem very willing to try to see your/their side of it), be consistent about making sure you and others get listened to and that your and their needs and wishes are respected too. This is essential, for everyone's wellbeing[i]. If there is resistance, be firm but limit yourself to brief statements that say a) how you or someone else might feel in a given situation, and b) observations/information about the situation. E.g. 'When I'm criticised I feel deflated.', and e.g. 'It looks like your sister is trying to say something.'

92. If your child tends sometimes to see things as black and white, or to blame you (or other family members) for their difficulties or negative feelings: try to be neutral but firm. The message you want to get across, loud and clear, is: 'Me and you are two different people; *of course* sometimes we are going to want different things, or see things differently'. Make it clear that this doesn't mean anyone's to blame, and it certainly doesn't mean you stopped loving them! You can also add that of course you're not perfect, by any means, in fact sometimes you make a right pig's ear of things, but you're doing your best. Every one of us

---

i   Not least your child's. It is really scary for children to be given this kind of power, even if it *seems* to be what they want (actually power over your family also means responsibility for what happens to them, and I think that's far too large a burden for a child). It seems quite likely they are actually desperate for something else – maybe reassurance that it's okay to relinquish control, and that nothing bad will happen if they do. So being firm should be accompanied by obvious unconditional love of the person themselves, and no blame or character judgements ('you're selfish', 'you never consider others', etc... I think all these kind of judgements and accusations are really counter-productive in this situation, not to mention totally irrelevant!).

messes up sometimes, it's an unfortunate part of being human. So, the emphasis stays firmly on *loving each other* and each person *doing their best*. If you can manage to then jointly find compromises to your differences in beliefs or needs: now there's an achievement[i].

93. If it feels natural, try suggesting possibly appropriate things to say in certain situations (sticking to a neutral or humorous tone). However, avoid doing this in front of people, or putting on any pressure to actually say the things; it can just remain a suggestion you dropped in there, in case they might ever find it useful.[ii] Another thing you can do here is telling anecdotes about your and other people's conversations and experiences.

94. Indulge in interesting conversations with your family members, e.g. at table or on walks. Make sure all contributions get listened to and considered.

95. Be aware that your autistic child might have difficulties with metaphors and figures of speech, and a tendency to take

---

i My impression is that reading fiction is fantastic for avoiding black-and-white thinking. I notice my children thinking deeply and asking questions e.g. when one of the characters has done something that annoyed the others and is in the dog-house, and the friends find a way of making it up. Or when the characters are discussing together what to do next and how they each have different ideas and thoughts that contribute to a mutual outcome. However, I would strongly recommend sticking to *good, real* fiction... not simplified stories produced on purpose to 'teach' children something, and even sometimes coming ready-packaged with questions that children are supposed to answer, about what *we* think they should have noticed or learnt about the story. The child *must* be left free to make their own observations and build their own ideas. Answers to questions (their own, real ones) should be brief and to-the-point, unless more information is requested.

ii Here is my all-time favourite, from when my son was about four years old:
Me (after some minor accident involving me and him, I can't remember what it was): 'You know, you *can* say sorry to someone, even when you didn't hurt them on purpose.'
My son (with great seriousness and clarity): 'Sorry, mummy. I did it on purpose.'

things literally. You can help by explaining any idioms, and/or having fun using some very silly humour (maybe saying totally exaggerated things so they can get the idea that this is NOT true but rather just really ridiculous and crazy things you say when you want to share a joke with people, or for super-special effect!).

96. Spend time in companionable silence, either working together on a project or just alongside each other, each busy with their own work. Personally I love working in this peaceful way with other people (pruning trees or picking fruit, painting model figures, cutting out cookies, shelling peas, building Lego™ models and finding pieces, etc. – the list is endless).

97. Play family parlour games like charades, consequences, acting games or guessing games. We also play a game we called 'emotions' e.g. when travelling on a train[i].

98. Keep any medication on as low a dosage as possible, trying only one thing at a time, and only using it if absolutely necessary. Avoid both long-term use and increasing the dosage if the effects seem to lessen. Inform yourself thoroughly about any medication you are thinking of giving to your child. Carefully document usage and how your child is responding.[ii]

99. If your child needs to go into hospital for any reason, and in particular if they need to stay overnight, make sure you let the staff know that your child is autistic and emphasise the

---

i   The person acting can go to the next bench and with only their eyes showing above the seat, act something (a reaction to something, a situation, an 'emotion' like 'anger', 'cheekiness' etc). If it's impossible to guess then you get to see the whole face, before moving on to clues and acting out small scenes. There are lots of games like this you can play while travelling. 'Animal, mineral, vegetable' is another good one.

ii   This advice is based on the suggestions of Temple Grandin, Lorna Wing, and Tony Attwood, who make practical suggestions about taking medications, based on their personal and professional experiences (see the Reading List). I have no direct experience, but I think this topic is too important to be left unmentioned.

importance of you or another close family member staying with them, being told what is happening and what is going to happen (and then you can give the necessary information in an understandable and palatable way to your child), and keeping your child feeling safe and reassured to the greatest extent possible (in particular when they're going under a general anaesthetic). These are reasonable demands, so be insistent if there's any resistance about them being met.

100. Try to arrange getting some time off. It is important that you get regular slots of time (ideally even an entire day sometimes) when you are responsible for no other person but yourself. This is good for your wellbeing (and therefore also for your family's), and also because stepping out of the thick of things, even for a few minutes, can give you a new perspective and some clarity on things that might be on your mind.

101. If you have doubts about specific situations and other aspects of parenting an autistic child, going onto autistic forums such as WrongPlanet.net can be really helpful. You can start a thread on your question, to see how autistic people respond (after all, who better to give some insight on what autistic children are likely to be experiencing?). You may well get some unexpected, resourceful and generally understanding responses and advice.

For those who are planning a baby, or pregnant

1. Try to make sure your pregnancy is relaxed, calm, and passed in a way that is as joyful and stress-free as possible. If at any point you feel that you are too stressed, or feeling very unwell or unhappy, try to find all and any ways that you might alleviate this, remembering to keep in mind the longer-term perspective whenever you consider your priorities[i].

2. If you can, during pregnancy do some yoga for pregnant women. In particular the breathing (and articulation[ii]) can really make the difference between a good birth experience and a not so good one. Ideally, during birth, someone should be present who can support you in the breathing, articulation and rocking.

3. Go to the hospital while you are pregnant (even if you are planning a home birth, it can be good to find out about the local hospital and procedures just in case you did happen to be brought there for whatever reason). Meet the midwives, ask about standard procedures, and who you're likely to get at different times[iii].

Some important questions are:

- Is inducing done only if the mother or baby's health are seriously at risk?
- Are epidurals given only on my explicit request, and in consultation with me?
- Will any medication (inducing etc.) be given to me without my explicit consent?
- Can I move around during labour *and* birth, or will I be obliged to lie on my back on a bed?
- Is my chosen companion allowed to stay with me the whole time?

---

i   Stress during pregnancy is known to have an impact on the developing brain of the baby, due to overexposure to stress hormones.

ii   This means saying 'aaaaah' loudly and deeply on your out-breath. I know it sounds very weird, but it *really* helps ... maybe because it stops you from screeching 'eeeek!' and forgetting to breathe altogether?

iii   This is assuming you don't have one-to-one care, i.e. being followed through pregnancy by the same midwife who will assist you during birth (which in most cases is the best possible scenario).

- After birth, is my baby allowed to stay with me, or will they be taken away and if so, for how long exactly and for what purpose?[i]

Make sure you bring a notepad along to write down the answers. If you're not satisfied, try to look for alternatives. Ask at your yoga class, ask friends who've given birth recently.

4.   Find the time to read up about other women's experiences, and write a short description of your own ideal birth (your 'birth plan'). See if you can find a way to have your midwife/s read it. This may make for more understanding between you, and an easier birth. If you get a bad feeling about your midwife, if she's unfriendly and making you feel stressed and judged, try to insist on getting someone different. This is why it can be so important to meet the key staff in your local/chosen hospital beforehand, as during labour this is just the kind of stress you really *don't* need.

5.   When the moment arrives, bring your favourite pillow and blanket to hospital with you. It sounds silly but it *is* reassuring!

6.   If you feel under any pressure by the medical staff to be induced, perhaps your companion can be primed beforehand to check that there are valid reasons for this. Being induced can significantly change the birth experience, as contractions are more likely to be erratic, and can start off significantly stronger than the first stage of contractions during a natural birth (a gradual build-up, which you have time to get used to, generally makes for arriving at the actual birth in a better condition emotionally and physically)[ii].

---

i   I think it is hard to imagine how very traumatic this first separation from the mother might be for a newborn infant. There have to be very good reasons indeed for it to be justified. The stress induced from separation, in particular if prolonged, can impact the healthy development of a newborn's neurological processes (for more information on this I would highly recommend Sue Gerhardt's book *Why Love Matters: How Affection Shapes a Baby's Brain*, see Reading List).

ii   Perhaps it could also make a difference to the baby's experience of birth, as in a natural birth the mother takes the hormonal cues from her unborn baby.

When you're induced it becomes more likely you'll need an epidural, and statistics show that the odds of birth by emergency caesarean also go up. Sometimes, unbelievably enough, contractions go away during a natural birth for long enough for the mother to actually have a rest or even a short sleep – which might be much better for mother and baby than being induced at that point. However, if there are clearly strong medical grounds for being induced (i.e. if your or your baby's health are at risk), then of course it should be done.

7.   Have plenty of drinking water on hand, and possibly even some light snacks in case you need them to keep your strength up.

8.   If you do have a caesarian, or need an epidural and other interventions during birth, that's absolutely fine. If you feel you 'failed' in any way, and if you're made to feel guilty by anyone or anything, reassure yourself! The fact is that birth for human beings is physiologically more complex than in most animals, and that's why we need so much help with it. It's overall an amazing and obviously life-changing experience, but every birth is completely different, and no-one can have a clue about what another person's experience was or is going to be. So any judging or feeling bad is definitely out of place here.

After your baby is born

1.   Insist that your baby sleeps with you in hospital, not in a cot and definitely not in a different room. They need to be cuddled, held and carried. Very small babies are unable to move their own bodies much, and they need some moving around for comfort, exercise, and to aid digestion – but as well as this, they need body contact to feel peaceful, warm, cared for and loved. Also, if you are sleeping next to your baby, you are sensitive to their movements, breathing and sounds they make, so you are more likely to respond instinctively with providing what they need.

2.   If anyone talks about the dreadful consequences of 'spoiling' your newborn baby, be polite, but discreetly leave their advice on the doorstep when entering parenthood...

3.   Resist any pressure to put your baby on a feeding regime[i].

4.   If your list of baby equipment to buy includes a playpen, please hold on that. For learning positive exploration of our world, starting inside the home, playpens are counter-productive, and can in fact bring a child to feel that very isolation and alienation which we are trying to guard against.

5.   Use a sling/baby carrier (often a simple long cloth is the best), as this can soothe your baby wonderfully when they are stressed, grouchy or tired. Encourage your partner and other close family members and friends to take turns, to give your back a rest and so your baby gets used to being soothed by others, not just you.

6.   If people say you shouldn't carry on having your babies sleeping in the same bed as you, as you're 'teaching them bad habits', again try to take it lightly. Most babies will graduate to their own beds quite happily in a year or two, and for those who don't, and continue to appear as if by magic in your bed every night, there is surely a good reason for it (see page 91 for a grandmother's wise advice). Maybe you could draw the line at them kicking you all night (literally – a bolster perhaps?).

However, while you shouldn't let public opinion dictate to you on this, if it's really driving you crazy (or if you find yourself looking at your husband thinking 'do I remember you?'), try to think of some alternative solutions, like allowing the dog to sleep on their feet in bed, or having a comfy armchair in your child's room where you can sit for a while when they feel insecure or have a nightmare (it should be VERY comfy and equipped with a nice warm blanket).

---

i   The main reason why this is very important, is that among the worst things you can teach to a new baby, in particular one with autistic tendencies, is that they have no control over their own fate. If their signals to tell us they are hungry, or even cold and wet etc. (they signal by crying, or if you are nearby and available they might just grunt, nuzzle or whimper a little) are ignored, they can learn to distrust the outside world and IN PARTICULAR to mistrust any influence they may have had on it through their own actions. This is absolutely not conducive to developing self-determination and self-regulation, and could even inflict lasting damage.

Don't

1. Use punishment to prohibit specific acts or behaviours[i].

2. Use rewards (also known as 'positive reinforcements') including praise, in order to elicit certain behaviours[ii].

If these first two points leave you floundering in a sea of 'what *am* I supposed to do, then??', I would highly recommend two books by Adele Faber and Elaine Mazlish: *How to Listen so Kids Will Talk, and Talk so Kids Will Listen* and *Siblings Without Rivalry*. They are full of excellent, practical advice, even down to cartoon strips showing real-life scenarios in the home.

3. Give love and approval on a conditional basis.

4. Criticise, put down. There are other ways to effectively demonstrate preferred ways of behaving[iii]. Usually the best way is by modelling, though positive suggestion can also be useful.

5. Indulge in constant correction. It's unnecessary and eats away at both self-esteem and joy of discovering about life[iv].

---

i   The overriding principle of the conference 'Celebrating Autistic Culture', arranged by and for autistic people (and described in *NeuroTribes,* see the Reading List), was 'opportunity not pressure'. I think this is rather a good approach for encouraging autonomy, confidence and self-determination.

ii   Alfie Kohn's book *Punished by Rewards* gives a thorough analysis of this. In any case, it's possible you may find (as I did) that your child doesn't always seem particularly gratified at being praised, sometimes responding in rather surprising ways and leaving you a bit perplexed.

iii   Though ask yourself searchingly, if what you are asking for is really desirable or necessary, and aimed at the longer-term well-being of your family and child. Anything with motivations such as social embarrassment, other people's expectations, or conformism for its own sake, examine whether it is really necessary to try to change behaviours. A general rule can be to ask yourself 'is it harming anyone?'. If the answer is 'no', reconsider making it an issue.

iv   A didactic approach to parenting really does not invite friendship and relaxation, and greatly inhibits your enjoyment of being together. Ironically it also has the effect over time of diminishing your child's natural enthusiasm for learning.

6. Compare unfavourably to others, or extoll the virtues of being outgoing, sociable, outspoken, or anything that your child clearly is not.

7. Put your child into obligatory social situations, and groups/crowds where there is no option for getting away.

8. Regularly expose your child to people who overtly dislike or disapprove of them, and who don't appreciate their qualities.

9. Regularly persuade or force your child into doing things (where avoidable) where a specific wish has been expressed not to[i].

10. Enter into battle mode with your child, i.e. a situation where you range yourselves against one another. You're on the same side! If you feel this happening, look for help and advice[ii].

11. Respond in an angry or negating way to emotional

---

i   Your child will challenge themselves and branch out when the drive comes from within, not from others (though opportunities and a conducive environment are essential). The long-term effect of external pressure is actually to inhibit self-motivation.

ii Again, the books are *How to Listen so Kids Will Talk, and Talk so Kids Will Listen* and *Siblings Without Rivalry*, can be very helpful in this.

outbursts – instead try to a) remove distressing factors, and b) understand the cause[i].

12. Support or agree with other adults (e.g. teachers or other parents) when they put down your child, or place blame or judgement on them, especially in their presence. Obviously you do not have to say 'it wasn't him!', if it clearly was – you could rather say 'I'm aware of what happened, and I wish it hadn't. However, can we focus on ways that we can improve the situation in the future, or reduce stress and tension overall?' (and you could suggest some practical ways you think might improve things for everyone, and prevent certain situations from happening again). If you find yourself up against a wall, having tried all the avenues you can think of without getting any helpful response, perhaps it's time to consider looking for other options for your child.

13. Shush your baby or child when they cry. It's better not to teach young children that feelings should be smothered, and that showing you're sad is not okay. Much better to rock gently, sing, say encouraging things like 'there there, I'm here love, aww poor one', and so on[ii]. If it's obvious what's upsetting them, you might say something like 'Gosh, that was a big bump', or 'Long journeys are exhausting, aren't they?'

14. Say 'ew' or 'yick' when you change your baby's nappy/diaper. In fact better to coo, and smile, and make some eye contact; maybe sing or chat to your baby. Changing should be a positive and caring experience; an opportunity to enjoy the love and intimacy between you.

---

i   Anger comes from pain and hurt. This is useful to remember in frustrating moments, and it is very important that your child understand that their pain and frustration always has a cause i.e. can be validated, and then it can be processed and dealt with instead of being internalised and manifesting itself in withdrawal and destructive feelings towards themselves and/or the world.

ii   Try to not mind what people think; in any case acting because of 'what people might think' is not really advisable, as your baby will most likely sense the tension and yell more.

15. Buy a potty straight away, unless you are camping or the toilet is far away (i.e. purely practical reasons); instead try investing in a comfy reducer seat for your toilet[i]. Avoid putting too much pressure on your child to use the toilet instead of nappies/diapers, the best motivator is to take every opportunity to have your child not wear one (does your kitchen have tiles, not a carpet?). They will quickly become aware of when they go, and will observe how the grown-ups do it[ii].

16. Ask your child a lot of questions about people, situations and feelings, i.e. delve[iii].

17. Expose to cruelty or bullying. Follow your gut feeling on this one, there are many good indicators when your child is

---

i   I realise that experiences may differ on this; I've observed that in our family the children generally seem to want to copy what the grown ups do, and the fact is they see us using the toilet not a potty (me not actually being willing to lead by example on this one).

ii   However if they won't go except in a nappy even when older, you could try gradually making the change by bringing them into the bathroom while they go in the nappy, then encouraging them to sit on the toilet while doing this, then make the nappy looser and looser, until is it just draped on the seat. At any step, if there is great emotional resistance, try just going back a step or two and starting again (this is a suggestion that I read in Lorna Wing's book *The Autistic Spectrum*: it sounds to me like a very good and sensible strategy, and clearly one which was often successful). Another strategy, which worked for friends of ours, is to spread some newspaper on the bathroom floor and let your child stand over those (it might be a question of posture, and being used to eliminating standing up). Try really hard not to show frustration or annoyance (aarrgh!!), and certainly never show disgust or disapproval! It's terribly important not to evoke shame around this issue, as this has the potential to create problems (including quite serious medical ones), later on.

iii The effect can be to make the child clam up where they might have later spontaneously and in their own way given you information. In any case, it's very unlikely they'll know what you're getting at and even more improbable they'll feel like talking about and analysing social situations and their feelings about them! It also indicates that you are worried/anxious, which increases the pressure to 'perform'.

suffering from bullying when you aren't around to deal with it (e.g. at school or nursery)[i].

18. Always keep your phone on. Instead, give priority to being fully with your children, listening to them, talking and laughing together.

In particular, try not to interrupt your children by pulling out your phone whenever it bleeps (unless you are waiting to hear from a very sick relative), and you can enforce, and lead by example, a 'no phone at the table' rule when sitting together, whether at home or out. At home your phone could be kept in a certain spot, to be occasionally looked at or answered – rather than in your pocket (or in your hand).

19. Be hurt and offended if your child doesn't always respond to your emotional needs – or respond at all if their mind is elsewhere.

Yoo-hoo!!

Do I know you? oh, hi Mom.

20. Place too much importance on being smily and chatty in social situations. Some people are better at listening and appear

---

i   Don't forget that institutions are understandably very likely to either deny there's any serious problem, or put it onto the individuals concerned, rather than say 'Thanks so much for pointing it out. Gosh, it does start to look like this problem is endemic to our community (if not our entire social system), so I guess we'll need to address it as a structural issue'. Hmm.

more serious than others. You can make it clear to your child that it is perfectly acceptable to be an observer[i].

21. Assume your child's best friends must be other children. Often their friendships with adults can be just as important.

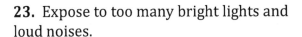

Yikes!

22. Put pressure on your child to compete against others. Competition is likely to be damaging to extremely sensitive individuals, whether they win or lose, as they sense any hostility (even when it's hidden) and are sensitive to the pain of others[ii].

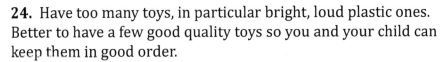

23. Expose to too many bright lights and loud noises.

24. Have too many toys, in particular bright, loud plastic ones. Better to have a few good quality toys so you and your child can keep them in good order.

25. Expose to disturbing films, images, or stories about people (in particular animals and children) being severely hurt or badly treated. Your sensitive child will do better without receiving too much information about anything cruel or unusual (especially visually), regardless of your ideas about the

---

i Susan Cain's presentation *The Power of Introverts* (Ted Talks, www.ted.com/talks) I think gives a bit of perspective on this issue.

ii I realise that this is a controversial issue. However as not all societies are by default competitive (instead favouring cooperation), it would appear to be a question of how our society has developed, rather than, as popularly presumed, a preset of human nature. I would highly recommend Alfie Kohn's book *No Contest; the Case against Competition*, for an evidence-based analysis. In addition Charles Eisenstein's book *The Ascent of Humanity* gives a lucid and beautiful account of how humanity has developed to the point we are at now, while refraining from dogma, judgements and political bias.

importance of staying informed about current affairs, or seeing the latest films in order to be up-to-date with peers[i].

26. Keep routines inflexibly. In fact, getting used to different places, people and things, while keeping a stable base of loving relationships, can mean your child doesn't get too fixated on sameness. Things can sometimes unavoidably change in life, so long term it's much better to have real inner stability and not be relying too much on external things which might get lost or broken, and on restricting and sometimes burdensome routines[ii].

27. Be *too* well-prepared. Don't panic if you've forgotten things; rather try to cheerfully make do with what you have. A parent who always carries everything one could possibly need makes for children who can get very fixed to the notion that you must have those things in order to be okay, and that it's a crisis if you don't.

28. Say 'it's not that bad', or 'but you have to see it from their point of view', if your child goes off on a rant about someone or something. Your message may sound really positive and moderate, but that's deceptive. Its real effect is to be absolutely infuriating to the recipient (thereby making them look even worse), while allowing you to feel rather good about yourself (what a superior human being

ARRGHH!

---

i   However, honesty and openness about natural phenomena such as death and reproduction, in the right moments, are essential. If for example a beloved animal were to die, I believe it is better for your child to understand this, and even be involved in a burial (for example), rather than to have the pet disappear and then only vague, confusing or inadequate explanations be given.

ii   Though it is important to be respectful of your child's feelings, and try to keep a good balance in order to maintain equilibrium and avoid everyone getting too stressed. If making changes will result in any distress, introduce them at first gradually, step by step, and focusing very much on the palatable and positive until your child gets used to idea of being okay with change, even on a small scale at first.

you are!). It also expresses underlying disapproval at their outburst. So the outcome is that they will quickly learn that it's better not to share their feelings of disappointment with you, and they will retain their bitterness. Try being understanding instead[i] – after a few minutes the ranting might conceivably become milder, possibly followed by a pause, and then 'hmm, but I suppose from their point of view...'

29. Physically restrain. Use every other means available, starting with respectful requests and explanations about things, in carefully chosen moments. These will bear fruit, so be patient. Do not grab or yank, or force hold, outside situations that are *genuinely* life-threatening. Do all you can to avoid situations where you feel there's no choice[ii]. If you think your child may seriously harm others or themselves, and you feel unable to cope with it calmly and preventatively (e.g. by providing alternative and less harmful outlets for negative and violent feelings), then a) look up any helplines that can be called in moments of crisis, and b) discover what welfare and health services there are locally. A therapist can sometimes be a good idea, but only if well chosen, preferably with the child's

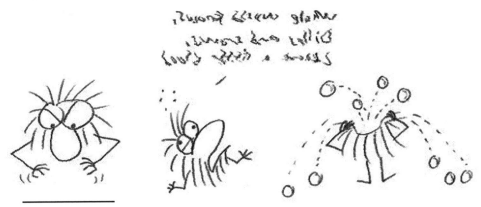

---

i   Again, suggestions for things to say are given in the book *Siblings Without Rivalry.*

ii Bearing in mind that the price to pay, if you have no choice but to use force, is likely to be the erosion of your child's trust in you, accompanied by their physical withdrawal from you.

consent (they should tentatively meet each other to see if they both get a good feeling), and taking great care not to give your child the impression that *they* are the problem. That's why I'd recommend it only if you feel there's no-one else in their lives able to give your child the necessary emotional support[i].

30. Live in a general state of unresolved conflict within your household, as you are likely to find that an autistic child will be acting as an amplifier (which will not alleviate your pain and stress, to put it mildly). If you are not living in relative harmony, fairness and honesty with yourself and other family members, it might be time to start considering carefully what can be done about it[ii].

31. Respond to anger with censure, for example requests to 'calm down', 'behave', or to apply self-control[iii].

32. Take it personally if your child's anger is directed at you. Listen and observe (without judging or disapproving), try to understand, keeping in mind that anger comes from hurt. As

---

i   The therapist should consider it their task to look for ways they can connect with and understand your child, and through this connection to help them come to terms with (and gradually reduce) their feelings of anger, pain, anxiety, and insecurity. If the therapist rather considers their main task to be 'improving' your child's outward behaviour, frankly I would advise finding someone else. Try to find a therapist who's genuinely kind and open-minded, who listens and observes well (children's play, actions and body language usually speak far louder than words) and who can assist in forming secure foundations which will help your child feel better about themselves and the world.

ii   I am not by any means suggesting that you never disagree about anything, or even that you don't have lively arguments! If anything, having a disagreement, getting upset or just showing and/or saying that you feel hurt, and then through two-way (or more, if other people are involved) communication getting around to understanding each other's point of view, which will then allow for figuring out solutions that can work to an acceptable degree for everyone, is great modelling for healthy conflict management.

iii If your child is unable to diffuse their feelings of anger through expression, it becomes a lot more likely those feelings will escalate. In other words, you may be dealing today with yelling, a mess on the floor, or a few thrown cushions. Or, if you categorically prevent and forbid that (without helping your child find other effective ways of expressing their anger and pain), you may be dealing with broken furniture, violence or suicidal thoughts in a year or two.

Don't

the primary carer, even if you are really close to your child and they trust you, angry feelings may be directed at you as the closest person they have, and getting on the defensive isn't going to help much[i]. If you deny the feelings any outlet in your presence (or failing that, with another trusted adult figure in their lives), this could do a great deal of harm, as your child could easily direct the hurt and anger onto themselves instead.

So what *can* you do? Maybe start by making it clear that you're not going to judge them or stop loving them just because they're raging and rampaging – let them know you recognise their feelings as legitimate (which they are, like all feelings, even though they might be projected) and then help find effective and creative ways in which the anger can be expressed, that work for them and are not harmful either to themselves or others, so examples could be pillow fights, creative expression (e.g. playing an instrument; drawing pictures of how angry you are[ii], dancing wildly round the living room to *The Clash*), running and yelling like crazy, or flinging stones as far as you can into the sea. Anything that works and doesn't hurt!

You may find that once the anger has been accepted and given a chance to vent, it slowly lessens[iii] and might now give way to grief

---

i   Also, I'm afraid that as tempting as it is to demand of your child 'Why? *Why?!?*', I think it usually does a lot more harm than good, as chances are that your guess is as good as theirs, and your underlying message is actually something along the lines of 'What is *wrong* with you??'

ii A suggestion given in *Siblings Without Rivalry*. I never thought it would work, but at times it really has done for us! You can show your child how to do it (no need for instruction), by doing it yourself next time you're angry. Don't hold back!! Take it seriously while you're drawing, even though it will often end in laughter.

iii However, if you are not managing to deal with and over time diminish their anger (which I believe is the result of painful and traumatic experiences, and of times when your child has felt betrayed, misunderstood, or hurt, at times by others and – let's face it – at times by you), seek professional help. A therapist may help you greatly in dealing with this constructively, especially since you are essentially acting as informal therapist for your child.

and open crying fits, or fits of nerves about day-to-day events. At this stage (basically when your child is approachable enough and trusts you enough), if it still happens sometimes that your child suddenly feels really emotional for no apparent reason, you can try things that might help them feel better (based on knowing them, observing, and past experience), making suggestions and tentatively trying different things. Maybe a head massage, or the floppy-legs yoga exercise (see p.23), or else making up a story or looking out of the window together imagining if there are people on other planets. Anything, really. The important thing is in one way or another to wind up each time with acceptance, friendship and understanding between you[i].

33. Force, coerce or pressurise into making affectionate or loving gestures. Be aware that your child may not be able to respond to your emotions (e.g. they may resist your embraces, or not provide comfort to you when you feel you need it)[ii].

34. Judge or blame. Often we dress up blame nicely in words like 'facing up to the responsibility' – beware of this. There are reasons for everything that anyone does, and placing blame on specific people helps no-one[iii].

---

i If you have to do this regularly, it's best you get some emotional support yourself – from your partner, mother, sister, best friend... or if none of those are possible (as it is important that they will not judge either you or your child), then see if you can find a parents' support group and/or a therapist. Online groups can also be great, but make sure you stick to ones where the overall tone is really supportive and tolerant, as it's likely you'll be feeling slightly on-the-edge!

ii You cannot force someone to feel something they don't. Leave complete freedom, while demonstrating your continuing respect and availability, and making loving gestures yourself when you sense they are welcome. If you sense they are not welcome, withdraw respectfully. If you feel resentful, talk to a friend or family member about it, or if those are not an option, try a therapist or counsellor.

iii It is more constructive to search for understanding and solutions/ compromises that will work for everyone to the greatest extent possible (and to succour any injured parties) than to figure out who's to blame.

Don't

35. Force to say 'sorry'. The best way a child can learn about really feeling sorry and being able to find ways of making amends to people, is by those around them modelling it.

36. Focus on an enquiry into 'what happened?' when your children have been hurt or upset during play (among themselves or with their friends) and you didn't personally witness what the cause was. Instead give your attention to the injured party ('are you okay? Where does it hurt?'), offer some comfort to them and possibly suggest another fun activity (e.g. 'shall we get the paints out?' or 'let's bake some cookies!').

If the child you suspect may have caused the upset then perks up and says 'can I play too?', hold NO grudges, just say 'of course' with a warm smile, and then you can spend the next minutes directing their play together into something more positive[i], and making sure everyone is being respected and treated kindly.

37. Force your child to do activities against their will, unless it's some family activity or outing which you are pretty sure will be fine for them, and that it would harm others NOT to go to[ii]. As far as possible, let them back out of things even if they 'promised' they'd do a thing or previously expressed a wish to (they may have not properly understood or known what it entailed). Contrary to much popular belief, real self-discipline and perseverance come from inside a person, not from someone else imposing it.

---

i   It may sound unbelievable, but if you do this consistently you'll find your kids (provided that there are not other major negative factors playing in their lives) begin to a) resolve their conflicts constructively without even calling you, and b) when someone is hurt, respond automatically 'are you okay?' (instead of 'it wasn't me!!').

ii   Although even in these cases, I would bring along books (or audiobooks), or colouring books, or maybe a model or puzzle to do, for a child who is not feeling sociable and would prefer to sit in a quiet place working on an individual project. Explain to any adults who are not naturally understanding about this, to help them be tolerant about a child's need for a bit of solitude and quiet time.

38. Give too many options, too frequently. Your child may be saying 'no' to things by default, even if they might want them, or you may be asking them to make too many decisions per day about things they don't care much about. You know your child, you know what's likely to be their feeling on many occasions (whether they like/want things or not). For example, at dinner (unless it's some dish we've never tried) I usually just go ahead and put food on plates, knowing more or less what will be eaten by whom.

39. Despair if your child seems not to be happy, cheerful or carefree, much of the time. Just closely observe what makes them feel better (look for the smile and the shining eyes), and what makes them worse (look for the downcast eyes, pale anxious face and hunched shoulders). Make a list. For a while, try to focus on only doing the things that make them feel good, avoiding the bad things. If there are areas you know are really important for them to be challenged in and to eventually develop a positive/proactive approach to, even though they seem to provoke anxiety in your child, then once your child becomes a bit more emotionally stable and positive, introduce those things/activities in small doses and in the most palatable way possible, and with plenty of the feel-good de-stress stuff in between.

Note: it can be useful to think of this as a *process*. If the overall direction is gradually towards more positive engagement, equilibrium and resilience, you're on the right track! It is absolutely normal that it might often seem like 'ten steps forward, nine back', or even at times that things have suddenly gone right back to awful again. Try to keep sight of the big picture! Keep a log for yourself if that helps, so you can see how things are going over time (how often are meltdowns occurring? How often are you seeing your child carefree and happy, and for how long? How many full days are you managing without major setbacks? When setbacks do occur, how long do they last? And so on)[i]...

40. Constantly override your child's natural sense of what is right and wrong, through correction, instruction and testing. Imagine a system that's in the process of developing and learning, and the controller continually applies 'override' when the system is still busy figuring things out for itself.
How far is that system going to develop, and how independent is it going to become?[ii]

No.

41. Read books about parenting that advocate a 'technique' or regime. Your instinct is likely to be a far more reliable guide[iii].

42. Say 'no' as a default. Make 'yes' the default, unless there are good reasons why not. Explain what those good reasons are, when you do need to say 'no'.

---

i   Peter Levine and Besel Van Der Kolk (see Reading List) both talk about the cyclical nature of human processes (i.e. when resolving and healing trauma), describing how 'expansion' (starting to feel good and confident again) is commonly followed by a natural 'contraction', often caused by some minor setback (oh no! Actually everything is awful, how could I have trusted it to be good?). This pendulum effect is standard – so it's important not to see every setback as complete disaster. I have a strong tendency, just like my son, to be 'all or nothing'. Things are either absolutely wonderful or totally awful. That means that there's a real danger of falling into abject despair over minor setbacks, which I can see does not do my family much good. Reading these books has really helped me to get perspective on this, and to be calmer when things go wrong.

ii   In his book, *How Children Learn*, John Holt describes this as 'sitting on a chair that's only just been glued, to see if it's stable'. Quote: 'When we constantly ask children questions to find out whether they know something (or prove to ourselves that they don't), we almost always cut short the slow process by which, testing their hunches against experience, they turn them into secure knowledge. Asking children questions about things they are only just beginning to learn is like sitting in a chair which has only just been glued. The structure collapses.'

iii   There are, however, many books that are not dogmatic or opinionated – instead tending towards being tolerant, kind, and realistic. I've included some of those I found most helpful in the Reading List.

43. Lie, or hide important information from your child (though of course you may have to tone things down sometimes if your child might be too hurt or disturbed by them). The child will sense untruths and be confused. If you feel you cannot answer or explain something, simply tell them so.

I did it!

44. Emphasise your expectations, and air your anxieties about your child's achievements in their presence. Try to trust that things will happen in their own time, and limit yourself to helping them build up a good foundation of security and self-confidence. You can however provide a good learning environment, and encourage contact with mentors, older children and other role models. Especially important and precious are relationships with adults and older children who clearly like and respect your child (and vice versa), and who really connect with them.

45. Avoid talking about autism. Instead talk openly and matter-of-factly about it, in situations that call for it or when your child asks you about it. Your child mustn't learn to be ashamed about who they are!

46. Push gender roles. Let your child act and dress in a way that makes them feel relaxed[i].

47. Pressurise into doing structured sports (particularly competitive ones), if your child has no explicit wish to do them. It's much more important to give freedom and time to explore and experiment e.g. they're interested in climbing? Instead of taking them to a rock-climbing course, try taking them to somewhere with walls, rocks, or trees, and let them roam. Bring your book and sit with your back to them. Refrain from giving suggestions or instruction.

---

i   Limit yourself to telling them if the situation they are going into is one where they may be stared at or judged – I think it is only fair to give a warning to a child who might very well find themselves being looked at and laughed at without knowing why.

Don't

48. Be goal oriented. Rushing from goal to goal is unlikely to be your child's style. Give them time and space to digest what's happening, to explore their surroundings, to follow up on interests as they feel the urge. In short, live in the moment and enjoy the process, look around you instead of keeping your eyes fixed on the distant horizon as you rush towards it[i].

49. Take it too seriously when people (especially when they are not family or close friends) say you are overprotective of your child.

50. Be blinded by authority. Psychologists, therapists, teachers and doctors have much valuable advice and support to give parents, but make sure you continue to think, analyse and research for yourself too (and remember, all of the above professional figures, if they're committed and creative individuals, will be open to exchanges of ideas and comparing of experiences[ii]). It is fine to question others' approaches and

---

i   Horizons have an annoying habit of receding.

ii If they instead tend to find ways of shutting you down, it could be because they feel that some of their basic assumptions are being threatened... perhaps they feel their boat is rocking a bit too much (though they may also simply be stressed out, tired, or having a bad day, and just want to go home!).

opinions – and in fact essential if you believe that the welfare of your family is in the balance.

51. Warn often to 'be careful', as it can have a paralysing effect. Your child may become fearful of some unspecified danger and unsure what can be done about it. Instead, give specific warnings only when necessary, and try to frame them as observations e.g. 'this is a very busy road'.

52. Overdo it on the 'health and safety' front. If given a chance to try (preferably without a grown-up hanging over them anxiously guiding them through every step), most children are perfectly capable of many feats that these days they are usually prevented from doing (e.g. using a knife, lighting a fire etc.). If given a good level of autonomy, they become agile with their bodies and hands, inventive and resourceful, and well aware of what they can do (and of their limitations). In the long run this is the way your child will become not only manually skilled; they will also become good at evaluating risks and making decisions[i].

53. Say it's nothing, or not to make a fuss, when your child hurts themselves. Try instead making sympathetic noises,

---

i   In our culture, we often emphasise our concern for the *physical* safety of our children, while having a tendency at times to disregard their emotional needs. I think this probably has more to do with how we legally deal with liability (i.e. how others can be held liable if things go wrong), than the true levels of danger and risk, and possible damage to the individual, which are attached to various things/activities. It's relatively easy to make the link and hold third parties to account when a child is *physically* hurt, while if the child is psychologically suffering because of factors in their environment or things that have happened to them, it's much more complex, harder to track, and of course nearly impossible to gather any empirical evidence on it.

Another thing to add here is that you might want to be cautious about making any warnings too strong/dramatic (e.g. describing in detail to your child the terrible things that could happen if you don't wash your hands after touching the cat, or if you were silly enough to drink the paint). Be aware that your child might be very impressionable and prone to developing real phobias about things, which will be hard to eradicate.

giving a cuddle (if wanted) and seeing if there's anything you can do to make it better. If your child refuses help or contact, stay close by but unobtrusive after saying 'I'm here if you need me'.

54. Hold unspecified grudges or give off an aura of disapproval (or *disappointment* towards someone). It's confusing and upsetting to others as it makes them feel bad without telling them what they can actually do about it. Try instead simply saying how you feel 'I'm really tired', 'I get stressed when we have to hurry', 'I hate getting in so late to a dark cold house'. With no blaming anyone, and no argument (no-one can deny how you feel, after all), it's quite likely you'll be freely given some sympathy and help.

55. Expect your children to notice if you need help in the house, or respond to your hints (or complaints) about it. It's better to just go ahead and ask for help. Be specific, direct and neutral. Reminders might be necessary, but again neutrally – avoid starting to plead or criticise at this point! Neutral one-worders are good e.g. 'Shoes' or 'Table' (pointing). You can also give choices, e.g. 'we need to feed the animals and lay the table. I don't mind, what's your preference?'. You can be flexible on timing if the job permits (but don't accidentally do it for them!).

56. Make rash promises to your child – they might have the memory of an elephant about those things (and remember at the MOST inconvenient moments!).

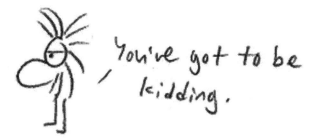

You've got to be kidding.

57. Swear at your animals (even if they pee on the carpet). Your child is likely to be a quick learner here, and might demonstrate their new skills in quite the wrong moments.

58. Poke fun at your children, or be even mildly disapproving, when they are exuberant, passionate or wildly enthusiastic!

59. Pressurise into taking a direction. Let your child meander and explore. You can provide opportunities, and a constructive learning environment, but you'll have little hope of finding the specific thing/s your child will love and be good at if you don't allow them to take the lead on this.

60. Take away treasured objects, or get rid of any possessions (including clothes, however worn-out!) without asking first. It makes the world unpredictable and unsafe. It's also not really respectful – imagine what you'd say if one of your family members did the same to you!

61. Assume that your child's acts and behaviour are done on purpose to annoy or manipulate you. Especially in very young children, and especially if they're having an expressive outburst of emotion, this is really unlikely to be the case[i].

62. Become a slave to carrying around ridiculously large and cumbersome objects, or to unrealistic and onerous routines, because your child tries to insist on it[ii]. However, a brutal 'no' might not be the best way to go about this; you can take gradual

---

i   Anyway, even if it were the case wouldn't we still need to ask ourselves why they might feel the urge to do it?

ii Maybe these obsessive regimes are because of feeling lost in the world, and therefore desperately clinging to things that might bring some stability; or fixating within a very limited and therefore possibly manageable sphere in order to block out the dangerous and unmanageable stuff as much as possible. What we wish for is to eventually achieve inner stability through safe, loving connections and stable relationships with animate beings (as human beings it seems we find this is necessary for complete fulfilment), so this is the foundation you are helping them build by being there for them and being understanding and accepting of them. Once any child has that foundation solidly built they are well equipped to manage pretty well in life, even in the face of adversity.

steps towards liberation, while all the while being loving, patient, but firm[i].

63. Regularly 'give in' to tantrums about wanting stuff (anything from ice creams or sweets, buying them their one-hundredth Lego™ model, to having other members of the family cater to random whims that unreasonably limit their own lives). As a rule, if kids can relatively calmly explain why they need/want something, or even if they just say seriously 'this is very important to me', within reason I would recommend doing what you can to help them out[ii].

However, if the request is accompanied by a sudden outburst of strong emotion you can feel reasonably certain that they are genuinely very upset, yes – but it's probably not about the professed thing, which wouldn't seem to warrant it. So, it's obvious that they are feeling awful. Maybe they are simply tired, hungry or overstimulated (especially with young children this is the first possibility to consider)? Maybe they feel that they are not listened to or taken seriously[iii], or perhaps that they're regularly put into situations they can't cope with where they feel powerless/ defenceless? Or maybe they reacted to a trigger which brought up some painful memory or past experience?

So, the way to react to this sensibly would be to first make it clear that you're not going to buy the sweets (or whatever it is), giving the reason why not, and making it clear this is not

---

i   Lorna Wing gives very good advice on ways to do this in her book *The Autistic Spectrum*.

ii As long as it harms no-one else. In particular keep an eye on the rights of siblings here.

iii Just thinking of families I know where you don't see the children having temper tantrums very often, I suppose it's not a coincidence that I'm observing people who appear to be in the habit of listening with a reasonable level of attention and respect to one other (and have enough time available in their lives to be able to do that).

up for argument right now. If they freak out, stay calm, sit with them or near them, having a cuddle if that's accepted, ignoring any unhelpful looks or comments from random people. When possible, see if your child is hungry, thirsty or tired. You could also calmly start pointing out passing things they might be interested in: you could try telling a story[i], or putting on their favourite song.

However, if (as is very likely) your time and/or patience is limited at that moment, arrange to dedicate a good amount of your time in the near future to doing something calming and gentle together, and if it seems appropriate, talking about any ways that anxiety and stress levels might be reduced overall (I like the Adele Faber and Elaine Mazlish method of brainstorming with your children – you write down all suggestions from both parties, no matter how wild, and then look through them together)[ii].

If you suspect that something or someone about the situation triggered off a strong reaction, make a note of this for future reference.

64. Automatically give sweets and treats to a child who's having/just had a meltdown, or give them your smartphone, or put them straight in front of the TV[iii].

65. Tell anecdotes about your child when they are present (yes, even stories which show them in a positive light!), without

---

i   If they're really angry with you (and you're the only grown-up present), maybe their teddy bear could tell a story if he has a voice... it's a well-kept secret, the usefulness of ventriloquy in parenting ☺

ii In all of this, the message you're giving is yes, you love them. Yes, you care, enough to dedicate real time and thought to them (and in fact in other circumstances you will listen and consider, if they show you over time how much they *really* want or need something). But no, you won't race about catering to frantic demands for random things that are highly impractical and inconvenient at that moment.

iii By doing this you're effectively giving an introductory course on how to self-soothe (or anaesthetise!) using food, drink, media or retail, as well as how to run away from and ignore/deny any painful feelings about things.

every time first obtaining their explicit and freely given consent.

66. Force your child to make eye contact with people. There are good reasons why autistic people find this difficult[i].

67. Say 'don't' (yes, I know! Blush!). Try clearly stated rules (which apply to everyone), e.g. 'shoes off at the door', or 'WiFi is switched off at so-and-so time',[ii] and/or giving information in a firm manner e.g. 'that tea is scalding hot', or 'this is a very steep slope'. Apparently a rather unexpected side-effect of saying 'don't', is that children hear the *expectation* in what you say (i.e. you're asking them not to do it, but your *expectation* is that they probably will). So you say 'don't touch the oven' and they promptly do so.

68. Be socially isolated. If you can, it's best to often be around people you like and trust. Maybe you can try to reach out to other like-minded parents in your area, perhaps setting up informal groups and regular meetings. If it's possible, it's great to be close to any of your own family members (siblings, parents, grandparents) with whom you and your children have a positive relationship.

69. Tiptoe around, close doors, and forbid visitors if your child sleeps lightly, and has trouble going to sleep. Instead your baby can nap in their pram in the kitchen alongside you while you cook, play music, or chat to your mum. If they wake, pick them up

---

i   I found Laurence Heller and Aline LaPierre's book *Healing Developmental Trauma* particularly useful on how to help and support anybody who has difficulties with eye contact (dedicating a whole section to it). And in the meantime, your child might find that there are certain tricks help them deal with eye contact in social situations – for example, they could look at a person's hair, or eyebrows.

ii At home you can attach your modem to a timer (maybe under a table in a dark corner) so there is always WiFi only for certain hours in the day.

and carry them on your arm for a bit. No need to make a big deal out of where or when they sleep. It may sound counterintuitive but sleeping well doesn't depend on silence: it depends on peace of mind, feeling safe, and WANTING to be asleep.

70. Use emotional blackmail[i]. This includes heavy sighs (for the benefit of those around you), and rolling your eyes, and reproachful looks at things like the dirty pots that someone else should have washed up. Instead, speak up! Some mild cursing and humour will work better than passive aggression and resentful self-sacrifice.

71. Use your children to try to make yourself look good (with a modest smile which says 'look everyone what clever/helpful/ obedient/athletic/etc. children I have!'). It will backfire on you[ii].

72. Put any pressure on your child to eat[iii]. Just provide regular meals and a pleasant environment, make sure you yourselves sit down to eat at every meal, and enjoy a chat together[iv]. Don't force your child to eat things they really don't like (they may have issues with textures, smell, etc.), just say 'eat whatever you can, and better not go on about the other stuff, so as not to hurt the cook's feelings'. Maybe serve things separately, as that can help. If your child really resists sitting up at meals, just sit

Oh, blech!

Blech, blech, blech!

---

i   Guilty, guilty! I have to consciously work very hard on myself not to do this.

ii Trust me. I've tried it.

iii As I see more children having problems with eating, it occurs to me – could it be a lack of control over other areas of their lives (including lack of unstructured time in which to develop themselves autonomously)? After all, the one thing you do have control over is what you put in your mouth!

iv Often at breakfast we look at books or make up jokes and stories. We regularly read books together at table, though I realise that's not for everyone. However no phones are allowed, especially not my own, as that's really not respectful to the people you're with (be they adults or children).

yourself down and enjoy the meal anyway, while not providing any snacks between meals beyond fruit. However if that doesn't work after a few days (not wanting of course to starve your child!), just go for *whatever works,* making as little issue out of it as possible while continuing to model enjoyment and pleasant mealtimes for yourself[i].

73. Worry too much if things go wrong, and you think afterwards that what you did or said was less-than-helpful (or totally disastrous, as the case may be!). It's really important to go easy on yourself – life should be as tolerable as possible for all those you care for, *not least* yourself. I watched a wonderful (and charismatic) presentation about compassion and self-forgiveness by a talented young man, Noah Britton, called *Autism: give me a chance and I will change everything*[ii], which might help you feel better if you're feeling a bit hopeless about yourself and your faults.

---

i   We currently have three rules at mealtimes. The first is that everyone has to stay at the table for at least 10 minutes (this was to counter the inclination of the children, when in the middle of some gripping game, to guzzle their food in 3 seconds flat – and refuse seconds only to be hungry again an hour later – in order to rush straight back to their game). The second is that if anyone is finding the noise level is too much and getting on their nerves, they can suggest a '3 minute silence' (using the egg timer). I've found it's amazing how you can really taste and enjoy your food during that lovely silence! The final (and I think most important) rule is that you don't moan or criticise the food, as unfortunately it's quite likely that the cook will get upset, on occasion even bursting into tears, and the mealtime will be ruined for everyone. If you really can't eat the food, don't (and yes, later – but only later – you can get yourself some bread-and-butter).

ii   Available on www.youtube.com

What about school?

Your child is likely to do better in a friendly neighbourhood-style school, where the children already know one another and where there is an overall benign atmosphere. If the teacher/s emphasise the importance of being kind to one another, and tend to monitor this closely and be firm about it, then so much the better.

If this is not possible, then **having at least one close, trustworthy friend** becomes even more crucial to your child's happiness. If you can find a way of being in contact with other parents of children in your child's class (ones your child likes), and socialising together in order to build their friendship, try to organise it. It could really be worth the investment.

If your child is already at the school, **is there a teacher/teachers with whom your child feels they really connect, and who seems to appreciate your child's qualities**? This could also make a world of difference to your child's school experience.

And here is a list of some of the questions you might find useful to ask about your child's school or potential school:

1. Can children (even young ones), when they feel the need, go to a quiet private place e.g. a relaxing room (possibly the nurse's room, if there is a quiet calming corner or space there), or a 'reading corner' in the library?

2. Is it obligatory to go outside with the other children at playtime, or can individual children or even a pair of children stay in the classroom if they wish to do so?

3. Are there special interest groups or 'clubs' available, perhaps in the lunch break? If these clubs are small and of mixed ages they can be great for children who feel overwhelmed by large rowdy groups of same-age children. It's also an opportunity for making friends.

4. Is there an adult in the playground at all times (and if the school is larger, what is the ratio of adults to children in the playground)? Do the adults present *actively intervene and* *participate* e.g. by initiating some non-compulsory structured activities in order to include children who may be feeling lost or left out?[i] For this purpose the activities should be collaborative rather than competitive e.g. building a hide-out, circle gymnastics and dances (for younger kids), building a fort in the sandpit, making an obstacle course. Whatever the environment permits (I know some are really challenging; it's not easy for teachers!).

5. Is there a mentoring system in place where older children are trained to help younger ones e.g. by befriending them, helping them find their way around, spending time with them in the playground (maybe playing ball, or whatever)?

6. Is there any greenery (grass and/or trees) in the playground?

7. Are there any school animals? Is gardening or caring for animals in the curriculum?[ii]

8. Can the sky and/or greenery (i.e. any *natural* light and scenery) be seen through the classroom windows (especially important if the children spend the whole day in the same classroom)?

9. Is there a sandpit, climbing frame, roundabout, slide etc.?

10. Is break time 'stepped', i.e. to limit the number of children going out at one time?

11. Are the teachers approachable, supportive and open to discussing and finding mutual solutions to difficulties?

12. Finally, does the school emphasise competitive spirit and achievement, or does it focus more on collaboration and the wellbeing and friendships of the children and teachers?

---

i   Many schools actually make a point of the fact that they leave the children to their own devices during break time, as this is a good way for the children to develop autonomy and have some free unstructured time. While I agree with this reasoning, I don't think it's a justification for not having sufficient adults monitoring *and intervening* on behalf of the vulnerable. There must be provision in place for children who lack friendship and protection. I think the novel *The Lord of the Flies* gives quite a good illustration of what might happen if a large bunch of children are left entirely to their own devices (that is, children who are used to a competitive style of education and upbringing).

ii   I know this is a long shot, but it's worth asking!

A note on trauma

If your child is showing signs of being traumatised by their current experiences[i] (typical signs of trauma in children to look out for are listed below, so if you see your child exhibiting a range of these symptoms together, chances are you can suspect persistent fear and trauma as the cause), it is best that you act immediately.

The greater the exposure, the longer the period of healing will need to be, and the harder it will be for them to recover. If you are in doubt, it is far better to *remove them from potentially traumatising influences* while you try to understand the situation.

Trauma in children; what to look for

Some of the symptoms of trauma in children are as follows:

- outward character change (what has happened to my lovely, happy, kind son/daughter??)
- extremely persistent, controlling behaviours
- school refusal
- pervasive interest in death and suicide
- sudden, very strong, and often seemingly inexplicable reactions to triggers/experiencing flashbacks
- sudden and frequent displays of extreme anger and agitation (e.g. meltdowns – ask yourself what happened just beforehand, and what the possible triggers might have been)
- chronic loss of appetite or overeating
- major problems with focusing on projects, school work, and conversation

---

i   The reason I specifically mention current experiences here, and not past ones (e.g. birth and hospital traumas in infancy) is because of the possibility of immediate action and prevention. For information on how to recover from past traumas, I would highly recommend Pete Walker's book *Complex PTSD: From Surviving to Thriving.* You do not have to be diagnosed with CPTSD in order to hugely benefit from reading the book.

- persistently disturbed sleeping habits, and nightmares
- chronic memory problems (e.g. extreme forgetfulness and short term memory loss)
- problems with speaking/verbal expression
- persistent regressive behaviours (e.g. bed wetting, 'tantrums', consistently needing a parent or teddy at night again, panicking about being left alone)
- extreme acting out in social situations
- imitation of the abusive/traumatic event (look out for signs like cruel treatment of pets or younger members of the family, as this can be your child showing you what has happened to them)
- persistent aggressive behaviours
- excessive screaming or crying
- a tendency to startle easily, and to be very nervous or edgy a lot of the time
- inability to trust others or make friends
- self-blame, self-hate, excessive shame
- extreme fear of being separated from parent/caregiver
- fear of adults who might remind them of the trauma
- persistent anxiety, fear and avoidance
- chronic sadness and depression
- withdrawal and immobility (extreme listlessness, aimlessness, and marked tendency to 'freeze' when afraid)
- extreme and persistent lack of self-confidence, feeling a failure and worthless
- persistent digestive problems, stomach aches and headaches

\|/

Here is a description of children who are suffering from trauma, given by the NCTSN (National Child Traumatic Stress Network):

> Children suffering from traumatic stress symptoms generally have difficulty regulating their behaviours and emotions. They may be clingy and fearful of new situations, easily frightened, difficult to console, and/or aggressive and impulsive. They may also have difficulty sleeping, lose recently acquired developmental skills, and show regression in functioning and behaviour.

Remember, it is not up to the parent or caregiver (or teacher, or other adults involved) to decide what the child *should* or *should not* find traumatic.

Every person's experience is unique, and whether or not the child suffers trauma as a result of certain experiences will unfortunately not depend on our opinion about what they should be able to cope with at their age.

Your child's ability to cope with the more challenging situations in their lives will depend on them gaining a healthy self-esteem and resilience, and on being equipped with a tool-box of good coping strategies.

\I/

The results of continued trauma are real, and can be devastating. Developing the necessary self-esteem and coping mechanisms which will result in inner stability (strength, awareness, flexibility and endurance, even in the face of adversity) is *not possible while the child is still in a chaotic state of panic due to ongoing duress.*

As a rule, the more and the longer the child suffers, the more severe the symptoms will become[i], and the harder and longer the recovery period will be. You will need every last drop of your patience and endurance in order to deal with the fallout, and bring your family back to emotional health – this is why I can't emphasise enough how important it is to intervene and halt the kind of trauma that can damage your child's developing psyche, if it is conceivably within your power to do so.

---

i   Bearing in mind that some quite severe symptoms, such as withdrawal and immobility or 'freezing', can tend to go unnoticed in institutional settings (certainly when compared with things like meltdowns and aggressive outbursts) for the simple reason that they usually don't cause anyone much trouble.

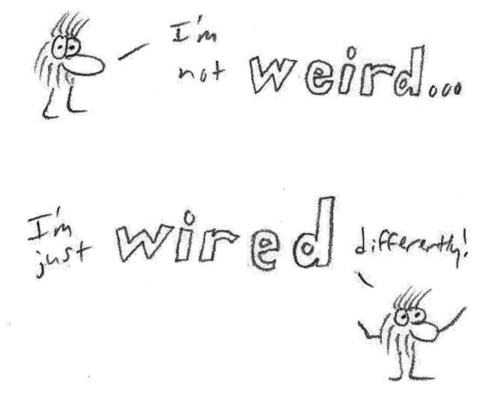

A bit of recognition!

Being a parent is such an enormous task that it's hard to know where to begin with this, but I felt I just had to add that I am very well aware of the difficulties in giving our children the kind of care and support we might wish them to have. And if your child is autistic – well, this seems to be the point at which we enter the realm of the unbelievable in how difficult it can become, but perhaps it's also the point at which many of us begin to question and change ourselves and 'how things are done', hopefully leading the way to real change for the better.

This is the reality: each of us is working mainly in isolation. Only the luckiest of families can manage on one income, or receive some kind of welfare support. But even those who have support financially, the fact is that we live in a world that does not value parenting or home-making as an occupation (either full or part time), and in which, when we do dedicate time to them, we are generally labouring away unseen and unrecognised in our little individual pods[i]. I do not find this an ideal arrangement, as there is usually no adult company, no friendly sharing of work among equals, and no respite (particularly if you decide to homeschool). No moment of freedom from responsibility and no real time off, not even at night. Add to that the usual comments you get when you've answered someone who asks 'what do you do?' ('um, what did you do before that?' and 'so when do you think you'll get back to work?'). Don't get me wrong, it's not them, it's our culture which educates us to so devalue arguably the most important job there is – preparing our kids for their time in this world, and for what they may do with it.

Besides isolation, another problem is that even if you do spend a lot of time with other adults, how many of those are your

---

i   While those who do also have to work for money in addition to this, will find themselves not just on night duty to look after their kids, but most likely also cleaning the bathroom at midnight, or sorting the toy cupboard before dawn (on no extra pay, and no recognition). How anyone can be patient and loving in such circumstances beats me!

real 'clan'? Do you trust them, love them, can you spend time comfortably in silence with them[i]? Because of the way the world currently works, we can't just implicitly trust everyone around us by default (not least because so many of us have had our own experiences that can easily result in us behaving cruelly, neglectfully or inappropriately to others, including children). The number of people with whom I would leave my baby is not high, even though I strongly believe it's best for babies and children to grow among people, to be held by others and not just their parents, to play and socialise with others of all ages, and later to be mentored by other adults and older kids (here's another problem – finding teenage or adult mentors who are relaxed in themselves, inspired and motivated, and loving what they do *right now*). Even if you do believe in the importance of community and sharing the load, it's a bit of a minefield.

So, it seems to me that what we are all suffering from to varying degrees is a deficit of real connection with others[ii] and of community (as well as lack of free time and time spent quietly and in nature). All I can say is that in such circumstances it is very difficult to raise our children with all the joy and humanity that we would wish them to experience now and in their future lives. So if you manage to achieve it even just a little (and with many lapses and confusions along the way), then you are not only contributing to your child's happiness and future, but to everyone – all of us, and to a more humane and beautiful world. Here's to you, parent and miracle-worker!

---

i   As long as competition remains the default, real friendships and alliances remain quite scarce. If you believe that human beings are always competitive by nature, maybe a trip to stay with the Bushmen (their own 'Living Museum' in the Kalahari Desert, gives the opportunity to do this), and reading *The Continuum Concept* (Jean Liedloff) and *No Contest: The Case Against Competition* (Alfie Kohn) may bring some doubts into your mind. I'd also highly recommend the documentary *The Economics of Happiness*, and the film *La Belle Verte*, which has the added advantage of being absolutely hilarious. I should mention that I also totally believed that competition is built-in, while kindness and generosity have to be learnt, but I have been taught otherwise by my own children.

ii Erich Fromm writes about this beautifully in the classic book *The Art of Loving*.

Afterword (Please, Miss!)

Only how can there be 'Dos and Don'ts', if autism is genetic?

There has been such a lot of debate about the causes of autism, and whether it is genetic or caused by environmental factors.

Having spent some time wondering what exactly is referred to when talking about 'autism' (and studied examples from many and diverse sources), it strikes me that we're combining two actually quite different things under the same term.

So, are we looking at:

1. Autism identified through the particular set of qualities we are born with? It seems to me that the principle defining characteristic of autistic people is that they are already possessed of often far higher levels of sensitivity than average (so that sensations[i] and corresponding emotions are experienced as being very intense[ii]), or:

---

i   Both from within the body or from outside it via our senses. All sensations experienced are communicated through the nervous system via synapses to the limbic system of the brain (the limbic system supports a variety of functions including emotion, behaviour, motivation and long-term memory), where they are interpreted emotionally and sorted for possible storage as memories. Memories can be either implicit (meaning they are only remembered as emotions or feelings; this is our only type of memory before the age of 2-3, as the part of the brain which encodes and recalls conscious memory, the hippocampus, is not yet fully developed) or explicit, meaning they are consciously remembered. A number of the genes identified as being relevant in the study of autism are involved in the formation and function of synapses.

ii So there is a risk that sensations and emotions, particularly negative ones, can be experienced as unbearable, or even traumatic, triggering a defensive shutdown. So paradoxically (as the capacity for intense feelings and empathy is so great) the end result might actually be a *lack* of connection with self and others. The Markrams' scientific paper *The Intense World Syndrome – an Alternative Hypothesis for Autism* (see Reading List) explores this in depth, looking at autism not as mental deficit, but rather a mental overload. The theory is backed up with a large body of research evidence.

2.   Autism defined as the problems and difficulties in life that are commonly experienced by people who possess this very high level of sensitivity (often when they are still babies or children), and the symptoms of trauma arising from their experiences[i]?

Once you separate the two things, it seems to follow that:

Number one is down to genetics[ii]. However, I think it would be reasonable to describe it as a way of being rather than as a 'disorder'. In fact, I can see there could be a number of clear advantages to high sensitivity, such as the capacity for enhanced creativity, perceptiveness, empathy and imagination.

Number two is by definition caused (and can fluctuate over time[iii]) by environmental influences in the individual's

---

i   The symptoms of PTSD are not dissimilar to those often seen in autism (see Appendix 1, p.83). For those interested in studying this subject in more detail I would highly recommend Besel Van Der Kolk's book *The Body Keeps the Score: Mind, Brain and Body in the Transformation of Trauma*, which combines looking at various types of effective therapies with giving detailed and comprehensible information on the neurobiological workings of fear, memory and trauma.

ii   Quote from *The Intense World Syndrome – an Alternative Hypothesis for Autism*, Markram et al., 2007: 'Not all children with predisposing genes develop autism indicating that the genetic alterations should not be seen as the cause of autism, but as a major predisposing factor.'. In the meantime, perhaps we need to question a little the popularly accepted distinction between 'genetic' and 'environmental'. While neuroscience begins to reveal clear links between people's trauma (and therefore predisposition to further trauma) and that of their children and even grandchildren, i.e. inherited trauma, research in genetics begins to reveal how our DNA changes (mutates) due to environmental influences (such as viruses, bacteria, parasites and symbionts) and how gene expression can also vary according to circumstances (and shows how the resulting traits can in fact be passed on through generations). So it seems to me that the line between 'genetic' and 'environmental' starts to look rather fuzzy.

iii   Tony Attwood talks about this is his *Complete Guide to Asperger's Syndrome*. Quote: 'There is now longitudinal research that is starting to confirm clinical experience that about 10 per cent of those who originally had an accurate diagnosis of Asperger's syndrome in childhood no longer have sufficient impairments to justify the diagnosis'. Their condition has in fact become 'sub-clinical', i.e. no longer diagnosable as autistic or Asperger's. In other words they have moved so far along the spectrum that they are now (clinically speaking) *off* it.

life, starting from the moment of conception. These could be anything from birth or in utero trauma, illness, allergies or reactions to toxins, to traumatic experiences usually in infancy and childhood[i] (these traumatic experiences might in some cases be caused or at least compounded by having to deal with some parallel disability or chronic illness), non-adaptive parenting and schooling methods, and lack of positive, nurturing surroundings and relationships. With one or more aggravating influences, we start entering into 'disorder' territory.

This would mean that most opinions about what caused or causes autism are validated. Yes, it is innate (though not an illness but rather a set of qualities). And yes, it is precipitated by environmental factors. It would explain why there are people who have the predisposing gene but are not diagnosed as autistic, and it would also make it perfectly possible (as indeed it is) for one identical twin to be diagnosed as autistic and the other not.

Of course there are environmental factors that are unavoidable (e.g. as mentioned above there can be health issues or disabilities coexisting with autism); in which case there is very little we can do even if we are aware of them. On the other hand, there are many things that we may have been assuming were unavoidable, which are actually not always so[ii].

This is the reason I have compiled this basic list of dos and don'ts, for parents and carers who are worried about those they love. I have a deep-felt wish that in some way I may be able to help improve the lives, even just a little, of some of the parents and children who might be affected.

---

i   Always bearing in mind that what is traumatic for one person, is not necessarily traumatic for another.

ii Perhaps we need to begin questioning a lot more things (about our lifestyle, upbringing, education etc.) than we are accustomed to doing.

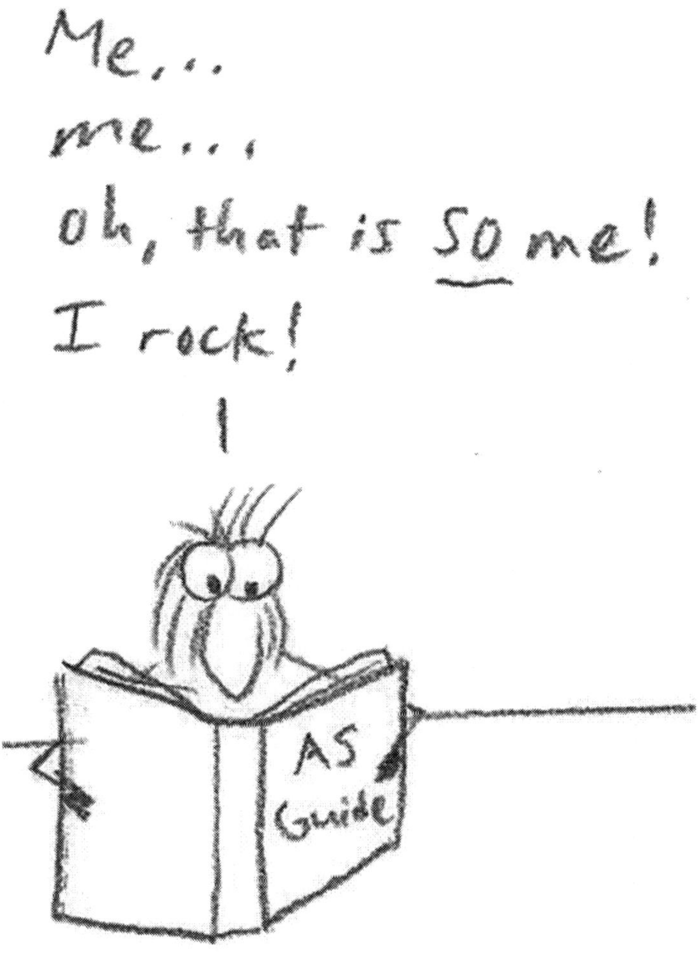
Me...
me...
oh, that is SO me!
I rock!
AS Guide

Reading List

These are the books, articles etc. that I have found most interesting and influential in my research. I realise they are quite diverse!

The Complete Guide to Asperger's Syndrome (Autism Spectrum Disorder), Tony Attwood

BBC IWonder: How does a child experience autism?, article presented by Carrie and David Grant http://www.bbc.co.uk/guides/zgdhwxs

The Ascent of Humanity, Charles Eisenstein

How To Talk So Kids Will Listen and Listen So Kids Will Talk, Adele Faber and Elaine Mazlish

Siblings Without Rivalry: How to Help Your Children Live Together So You Can Live Too, Adele Faber and Elaine Mazlish

Madness and Civilization: A History of Insanity in the Age of Reason, Michel Foucault

The Art of Loving, Erich Fromm

Emergence: Labeled Autistic, Temple Grandin

Why Love Matters: How Affection Shapes a Baby's Brain, Sue Gerhardt

Smart Moves: Why Learning Is Not All In Your Head, Carla Hannaford

Healing Developmental Trauma: How Early Trauma Affects Self-Regulation, Self-Image, and the Capacity for Relationship, Laurence Heller and and Aline LaPierre

The Reason I Jump: One Boy's Voice from the Silence of Autism, Naoki Higashida

How Children Learn, John Holt

Teach Your Own: The John Holt Book Of Homeschooling, John Holt

Never One of Them: Growing Up With Autism, Lance Earl King

No Contest: The Case Against Competition, Alfie Kohn

Punished by Rewards: The Trouble with Gold Stars, Incentive Plans, A's, Praise and Other Bribes, Alfie Kohn

Waking the Tiger: Healing Trauma, Peter A. Levine

The Continuum Concept, Jean Liedloff

Last Child in the Woods: Saving Our Children from Nature-deficit Disorder, Richard Louv

Nature Principle, The: Human Restoration and the End of Nature-Deficit Disorder, Richard Louv

The Intense World Syndrome – an Alternative Hypothesis for Autism, Markram et al., 2007. Abstract available at https://www.ncbi.nlm.nih.gov/pmc/articles/PMC2518049/

Children with Emerald Eyes: Histories of Extraordinary Boys and Girls, Mira Rothenberg

The Body Remembers: The Psychophysiology of Trauma and Trauma Treatment, Babette Rothschild

Scientists link 60 genes to autism risk, Danielle Ryan (CNN). Available at http://edition.cnn.com/2014/10/30/health/autism-genes-studies/index.html

An Anthropologist on Mars, Oliver Sacks

Reasonable People: A Memoir of Autism and Adoption, Ralph James Savarese

NeuroTribes: The Legacy of Autism and How to Think Smarter About People Who Think Differently, Steve Silberman

The Rosie Project: A Novel (Don Tillman #1), Graeme Simsion

Far From The Tree: Parents, Children and the Search for Identity, Andrew Solomon

Dumbing Us Down: The Hidden Curriculum of Compulsory Schooling, John Taylor Gatto

The Body Keeps the Score: Mind, Brain and Body in the Transformation of Trauma, Besel Van Der Kolk

Nobody Nowhere: The Remarkable Autobiography of an Autistic Girl, Donna Williams

The Autism Spectrum: A Guide for Parents and Professionals, Ms Lorna Wing

Complex PTSD (Post Traumatic Stress Disorder): From Surviving to Thriving, Pete Walker

The Child, The Family And The Outside World (Classics in Child Development), D. W. Winnicot

The Family and Individual Development (A Collection of Papers), D. W. Winnicot

Care in Normal Birth: a Practical Guide, World Health Organisation

And there are so many fascinating and relevant books and articles out there that I have not read yet! I'm still very much on the case, and I love to have recommendations about what to read next.

Appendix 1

Symptoms experienced by people suffering from Post
Traumatic Stress Disorder (PTSD):

- Limited imagination, and fixations (or 'obsessive behaviour')
- Lack of body coordination/fluidity (or being 'gravitationally challenged')
- Lack of expression in communication (gestures, voice intonation)
- Language skills affected, even to the point of being actually unable to speak (Broca's area of the brain)
- Strong emotional (right brain) reactions to seemingly insignificant things, and looking for someone or something to blame for them in the present
- Memory and attention impairments
- Disproportionate reaction to mildly stressful (for others) situations
- Being touched makes you want to scream
- Bowel/elimination problems
- Difficulty controlling emotions and impulses (due to shift of balance between the Amygdala and MPFC (Medial Prefrontal Cortex, what Van Der Kolk refers to as the 'watchtower' of the brain, while he calls the Amygdala the 'smoke detector')
- Depersonalisation (feeling like a detached observer of oneself)
- Dissociation (detachment from physical and emotional experiences)
- Alexithymia (inability to identify and describe emotions in the self, or 'feeling nothing')
- Lack of nuanced response to frustration (either all or nothing)
- Lack of, or difficulty with, eye contact
- Self harm and suicidal thoughts
- Sleep problems and nightmares

- Flashbacks as a response to triggers (often seen as seemingly inexplicable panic attacks, attacks of rage, or sudden withdrawal/immobility)[i].

These examples, with the exception of the last three which are from the US National Center for PTSD website, are given in Besel Van Der Kolk's book *The Body Keeps the Score: Mind, Brain and Body in the Transformation of Trauma.*

---

i   In PTSD triggers could become almost anything, especially if memories of unresolved trauma are only stored as implicit memories (sensations and emotions – this includes all memories up to the age of 2-3, i.e. before the hippocampus is fully developed and functional), as through ever lengthening chains of classical conditioning our brains associate simultaneously occurring things with one another (like Pavlov's dogs, salivating on hearing the bell, and then the bell itself can be associated with another thing like a light for instance, producing the same instinctive reaction – in this way the chains of association can go on and on, even when the original cause of the feeling is in the long distant and forgotten past. The reaction remains just as intense as it ever was, but is now seemingly inexplicable; apparently unlinked to anything even remotely rational. Through this mechanism fear and anxiety can grow to pervade every aspect of life, at which point it is recognisable as PTSD. Van Der Kolk describes this associated fear advancing and expanding until the person has ultimately developed an intense and paralysing fear of fear itself.

In their paper on autism, the Markrams talk about fear responses and this type of conditioning in relation to autism, having found that 'VPA treated rats store fear memories in an exaggerated and more persistent manner, generalize learned fear more easily to similar stimuli and once fear to a particular stimulus configuration is acquired it is more difficult to erase'.

Index

Hobbies 10, 28. *see also* Special interests

Holidays 10. *see also* Outings

Hospital. *see* Medical intervention

Housework 26, 27, 60

Humour 27, 37

Hurrying 15, 21

Idioms 36, 37

Inappropriate behaviour 61, 69, 70.
How to deal with 31–35, 50–53 *see also* Boundaries; *see also* Rules; *see also* Anger

Independence. *see* Autonomy

Inducing. *see* Medical intervention

Infancy 13, 14, 40, 41, 42, 45. *see also* Sleeping

Inflexibility 35–36, 49. *see also* Flexibility

Interacting 20, 24–26, 32, 35, 36, 46, 47, 60, 64. *see also* Relationships; *see also* Friendship

Intimacy. *see* Relationships

Kindness 12, 74. *see also* Acceptance; *see also* Consideration; *see also* Helping others; *see also* Tolerance;

Language. *see* Interacting

Laughter. *see* Humour

Learning 11, 16, 28, 30, 36, 43, 56, 61, 67, 68.

Light 9, 17

Literal thinking 35–37

Loving gestures 13, 53, 60. *see also* Affection

Massage 13, 23. *see also* Yoga

Mealtimes 65–66. *see also* Eating

Medical intervention 37
During birth 39–41

Medication 37

Meltdowns 15, 22, 50–52, 55, 62–63, 69. *see also* Anger
Avoiding meltdown 14, 15, 17, 18, 21, 22

Mentoring 26, 67, 68. *see also* Learning

Motivation
Self-motivation 17, 43, 44
Ways of increasing 10–12, 16–18, 20–21, 25, 30, 36–37, 57, 59

Movies 18, 28

Music 31, 63

Nappies 45

Nature 9, 68

Newborns. *see* Infancy

Nightmares 13, 42, 70, 83

Noise 17

Nutrition 18–19. *see also* Eating
Supplements 19

Obsessions 11, 83. *see also* Special interests

Optimism. *see* Enjoying life

Outdoors 9, 10, 12, 22, 57
Camping 10

Outings 9, 18, 22, 30, 33, 57

Overstimulation 9, 14, 15, 18, 21, 29, 62. *see also* Anxiety

Parties 21. *see also* Social life

About the Author

Katy Elphinstone has gone through various professional lives: working as librarian (for seven years, at the British Council in Rome, Italy), programme assistant (to the Regional Director for Europe at Bioversity International), freelance graphic designer and illustrator (for the UN and other organisations), and most recently web designer and editor (at St George's British International School in Rome, Italy).

She now lives with her family in the countryside outside Rome, and works full-time looking after house, garden, animals and family. However, her main and most important task is being responsible for the education and social life of two wonderful children (taking place in three languages: English, German and Italian).

About the Illustrator

Matt Friedman is a grant writer, fundraising professional, and cartoonist. He is the author and artist of *Dude, I'm An Aspie*, which depicts life with Asperger's Syndrome with honesty and humour, using simple yet effective cartoons that are way more powerful than words.

Grandmother's Wisdom

My mother has two most-used responses to many of the worries or doubts I or my sister have had about our children, or about parenting in general (this is besides giving us an enormous amount of practical and moral support). I find them possibly among the nicest and most helpful comments a grandparent could make. Here they are:

'Parenting is not really so much about what you* should *do, it's more about what you can endure.'

'He/she probably won't be doing it when he/she's fourteen.'[i]

---

i   You can change 'fourteen' to 'twenty-five', or even 'forty' if your child is already over that age.

Printed in Great Britain
by Amazon